THE BOY AND HIS GANG

LECTOR HOUSE PUBLIC DOMAIN WORKS

THE BOY AND HIS GANG

JOSEPH ADAMS PUFFER

ISBN: 978-93-5614-823-9

Published: 1912

LECTOR HOUSE LLP
E-MAIL: info@lectorhouse.com

THE WHARVES ARE A FAVORITE MEETING PLACE FOR THE GANG

THE BOY AND HIS GANG

BY

J. ADAMS PUFFER

Director of Beacon Vocation Bureau, Boston

ILLUSTRATED

1912

PREFACE

SIXTY-SIX boys who were members of gangs are responsible for this book. They told me the stories of their gang life and I wrote them out in the form illustrated in Chapter II. I showed these stories to President G. Stanley Hall, who asked me to present them in the *Pedagogical Seminary*, where an article appeared in June, 1905. These original stories of Boys' Gangs and Boy Leaders later became the basis for a series of lectures on Boy Problems. In revising my material for book publication, many interesting criticisms by parents, teachers, and social workers, in various sections of the country have been consciously or unconsciously incorporated into it. I have found a wide interest in and demand for such a book as this—bearing upon the group psychology of boyhood—and a lamentable scarcity of readable literature on the subject.

For aid in preparing this book I am indebted first of all to the boys for their confidence, which I have tried to keep; to President G. Stanley Hall for his kindly encouragement at the right time; to President Edmund C. Sanford and Professor William H. Burnham for pedagogical guidance; to my wife, E. Hope Puffer, who has shared in the task from the beginning; to Mr. E. T. Brewster for his invaluable assistance in editing the book, and to *McClure's Magazine* for permission to reprint the illustrations.

J. ADAMS PUFFER.

CONTENTS

LIST OF ILLUSTRATIONS

INTRODUCTION

THE gang spirit is the basis of the social life of the boy. It is the spontaneous expression of the boy's real interests. A boy must have not only companions but a group of companions in which to realize himself. This book had its origin in the minds and hearts of boys still active in their gangs.

It is evident that nearly all the activities of boys in their group life are not injurious but wholesome, or can readily be made so. What grown people too often interpret as done from evil motives the boys in the gang do from their love of fun. The educational world has not yet taken the interesting view point, that in the group activities of boys are cultivated the great fundamental virtues, coöperation, self-sacrifice, and loyalty. Now that we are coming to understand and realize what the gang life means, and what can be done with it, the surprise grows that it has until so recently been left almost entirely out of account in the work of helping and saving boys.

Mr. Puffer as a graduate student and fellow at Clark University has taken time to acquaint himself with the literature in this and adjacent fields, and as a practical worker has shown himself unusually sympathetic with boys and helpful to them. Mr. Puffer's writing is uniquely effective and his book ought to be read by all parents and friends of boys.

G. STANLEY HALL.

WORCESTER, MASS.,
February 12, 1912.

THE BOY AND HIS GANG

CHAPTER I

THE ETERNAL BOY

The nature of the problem, and the persons to whom this work is addressed.

We adults do not commonly understand boys. Half of us, to be sure, were boys ourselves; but when we became men and settled down to our work, we did not merely put away childish things—we went further and forgot them. To-day, we read a story of boy life and we say, "Why, yes. That's just the way boys do. I used to do exactly that sort of thing myself." But the next hour we have forgotten again, and the boy we were is once more a stranger. Boyville is so far removed, both from Delos and from Babylon, that we seldom think the thoughts of its inhabitants, nor see the world with the boys' eyes. Only a few men are at home in both worlds,—Lindsay, George, some schoolmasters, an occasional father,—and these can do anything with a boy.

The difficulty seems not so much to be that we have forgotten the incidents of our boyhood as that we have lost its feelings. So far as specific doings are concerned, we probably remember those crowded years more distinctly than any equal period of our entire lives. Most of us, too, remember them happily, as happily probably as any years we have lived. No, the trouble is not with the memory, but with the self. The experiences of life since we were boys have shifted our psychic centre of gravity, so that we realize the particular incident far more easily than we realize the being to whom it occurred. We do not completely feel that the boy that was is quite ourselves; and while the memory of the fact is sharp, the memory of the mental state that went with it has become dim. Therefore, it costs a distinct effort to put one's self in the boy's place. Any proper man will recite by the hour tales of the old swimming-hole in the summer. But if men actually felt toward the water as boys do, every club and half the private houses would have a swimming tank instead of a smoking room.

But if we men fail to comprehend boys, what shall we say of the women! The experiences which we have forgotten, they have not even had; if there is a psychic fence which separates men from boys, there are at least knot-holes in the boards; but between boys and women there is a solid wall. There are parts of a boy's soul which any woman may observe or imagine, but which no woman can ever feel. That women often do understand boys, understand them sometimes better than men do, is simply one of the marvels of feminine insight.

This book is, then, addressed, first of all, to fathers, with the hope that it will, in some sort, serve to revive memories of boyhood days, not so much of specific acts of boyhood as of long-dead impulses and past ways of envisaging the world. Every man who sits down and thinks out for himself, not only what he did as a boy, but also how it feels to be a boy, and how the world and the people in it appear through a boy's eyes, has taken a long step toward the understanding and the control of his own sons. A scientific account of certain aspects of boy psychology, such as this book aims to be, may aid this introspective process.

On the other hand, so far as this book is an account of the natural history of the genus boy, it may well be an aid to mothers, and to other women who, with no children of their own, are yet concerned for the welfare of adolescent males. If it does not help these to a sympathetic understanding of a boy's soul, one may at least hope that it will serve to warn them of those regions of it most foreign to their sex. Next to a knowledge of boy nature, comes the knowledge of when to keep hands off and let some man have his chance. To the smaller group of women, mothers and aunts and elder sisters, and especially teachers, who already possess the heaven-sent gift of understanding boys, any assistance may well seem superfluous. Still, intuition may often be supplemented by science. The clearest insight does sometimes fail, and need to be helped out by a more analytical approach from another side than its own. To men, women, and teachers, then, this book,—an 'apology,' in a sense, to women, of men who once were boys.

Whoever it was that opined that

"Men are but children of a larger growth"

knew little about boys. The child becomes a youth, and the youth becomes man, by virtue of a process not so very different from that which transforms the caterpillar into a butterfly or the tadpole into a frog. As truly as the caterpillar takes on wings, and the tadpole lungs and limbs, of which neither had any trace before, the child and the boy take on not only habits and instincts and ways of getting on in the world, but actual new structure as well. Boyhood begins with the second set of teeth; it ends with the advent of the beard and a new set of enzymes in the blood. Neither child nor boy nor grub nor pollywog passes on to the next stage of his existence by any mere enlargement.

Nor is it altogether true that with the approach of manhood

"Shades of the prison-house begin to close
Upon the growing boy."

The little child, in his father's house and under his father's care, feels the stir of newborn gregarious instincts, and takes his first steps into the larger life of the world. Boyhood proper begins with the rise of impulses which make us citizens and lead us to take care of ourselves; and it ends with the rise of impulses which make us heads of families and lead us to take care of other people. Each step is an enlargement of life. Each transition is marked by a psychic change so profound that it makes the previous narrower condition appear as shadowy almost as a dream, and almost as difficult to recall.

We are concerned here with the second of the seven ages of men: with the period, that is, which begins at about the age of ten with the rise of the herding instincts, and ends with the rise of the mating instincts at, say, eighteen. The child, who thus far has been a solitary animal, suddenly becomes a social one. He is profoundly interested in youth of his own sex, while at the same time he cares less than nothing for youth of the other. Therefore, he associates himself with other boys and forms gangs.

The gang, therefore, while it lasts, is for the boy one of the three primary social groups. These three are, the family, the neighborhood, and the play group; but for the normal boy the play group is the gang. All three are instinctive human groupings, formed like pack and flock and hive, in response to deep-seated but unconscious need. Like all such instinctive associations, the gang appears useless or stupid to those who have never felt the inner impulse which caused it, or who, having felt, have forgotten. The boy's reaction to his gang is neither more nor less reasonable than the reaction of a mother to her babe, the tribesman to his chief, or the lover to his sweetheart. All these alike belong to the ancient, instinctive, ultra-rational parts of our human nature. They are felt, and obeyed; but only in part are they to be explained, for no man understands any of them fully unless he knows how it feels from the inside.

CHAPTER II

THE GENERAL NATURE OF THE GANG

Importance of gangs— Their neglect in the literature of boyhood— The single conspicuous exception— The author's own experience with boys' gangs and its lessons— Boys' own stories of six specimen gangs— Fundamental likeness of all gangs— Their instinctive basis.

THE gang age, from ten to sixteen, is one of the most important eras in a boy's life. One man out often may belong to a church, one out of five to a fraternity: but as Sheldon has shown, three boys in every four are members of a gang; and the character of this gang determines in no small degree what sort of men these boys shall become. Taking our lives through, our parents probably make us most, and next to these our wives. But next to our wives, in their influence over our characters and careers, come for most of us, the group of companions whom we knew as boys and who together with us formed our special gang. Our domestic education takes place in our parents' home and in our own; but our social training has had at least its foundations in our gang.

Curiously enough, in spite of the fact that three quarters of all boys are members of gangs, the gang plays a somewhat inconspicuous part in the literature of boyhood. Neither in "David Copperfield," nor in "Being a Boy," nor in "A Boy's Town," nor in "Tom Brown," does the gang, *qua* gang, appear. There are traces of it in Owen Johnson's Lawrenceville stories, and in certain tales of Elisha Kellog, dear to the heart of a generation ago. Only one story of boy life, so far as I know, gives the gang anything like its full value in boy psychology.

This tale is "The Story of a Bad Boy" of Thomas Bailey Aldrich. The "Centipedes," to which the Bad Boy belonged, were a real gang. They had their local habitation, their badges, their ceremonies, their secrets. They went camping together, swam and boated and fished, snowballed the constables, fought the boys from the other end of the town, bombarded the sleeping inhabitants of Rivermouth on the night before the Fourth, and altogether comported themselves like the indefatigable young savages which all proper boys have been since boys were. The story is said to be highly autobiographical, to be, in short, the inside history of Aldrich's own gang. At any rate, it seems to be the most adequate account yet in print of a typical boys' gang, told with insight and skill. One can hardly imagine a better introduction to the ways of all boys than this story of a bad one.

Like most persons who were once boys, I was myself in my boyhood days a member of a gang; but I never began to realize the spirit and power of gang life until, between 1902 and 1905, I sat behind the Principal's desk in an Industrial School for Boys. Before that desk stood each new-comer, and it was my duty to place each boy in his school work, and to be responsible in part for his discipline. I soon learned that rightly to guide a boy in the School, it was essential that I know pretty thoroughly, not only the boy's personal traits, but also the social conditions of his home and of his neighborhood. I asked, therefore, many questions about home, school, and playmates, especially about playmates and the way in which the boys spent their leisure time.

Many boys, after a short acquaintance, told me freely the inside stories of their gang life. Occasionally, to start a narrator when he stopped talking, I would put in a question: "When do you meet?" "Where?" "What do you do nights?" "Saturdays?" "Sundays?" "Whom do you let in?" "Have you any rules?"—and the like. Where a boy had a good memory and a fair command of English, no questions were necessary; he simply went ahead and told me quite frankly all he knew, while I wrote down the story as nearly as possible in the boy's own words. Later when, as probation officer in a juvenile court, I became responsible for the behavior of dependent and delinquent boys, I carried the study further.

As a result of this information, it soon became evident that certain gangs were doing irreparable harm. Two boys, for example, out of one gang had been sent to the State Reform School on the same day; another contributed to the same institution, five of its six members. Good, promising boys, too, they were, though the world thought otherwise. Apparently, then, some gangs at least were pretty thoroughly bad.

On the other hand, some gangs proved to be almost as thoroughly good. Their members were real boys, but on the whole the gang was helping them to become worthy citizens and upright men.

I have especially full information concerning sixty-six gangs; and I pass without more ado to the boys' account of certain of them. Most men who read these pages can supply the inside history of at least one other.

The Morse Hollow Athletic Club

This is a typical all-round gang, though its main purpose was to play games. Its membership varied somewhat with the game, but it usually contained from nine to eleven boys, between twelve and seventeen years of age. Of these one was Irish, two were French, two Americans, one Negro, and one Scotch. The historian of the gang is the Scot, a distinctly bright boy who is now doing well at the printing trade.

"Met nearly every day in vacation time; had a shanty for a clubhouse over in the woods; met there most of the time; met on R. A's hill.

"R. A. was the leader. One that could jump the farthest was made president; one could jump next farthest, vice-president; next, secretary; one that could jump least distance of all was made treasurer; club was for athletics, so that was the way we wanted it.

"We played baseball in the spring and football in the fall. We didn't let a fellow into our club unless he could play baseball or football. Nights we would meet on the corner of the street and talk over games. We have been going together four years; we take in a new lot of younger boys every year. Sometimes we put a fellow out of the club because he will not pay his share of the expenses.

"Sundays we went to church; sometimes we would go up on R. A's hill in the afternoon and watch some men play cards for money; they gave coppers to the boys.

"We often jumped a freight to Gates Crossing and then went berrying or after nuts. We used to play Indians in the woods; one boy captured the others and put them in a hole. We had three detectives. We stole some apples out of orchards. We had a fight with the 'Garden of Eden' gang; we were coming home from football; we guyed them for beating us; they fired sticks at us; we made some swords out of wood, got an air rifle, and made an attack on them and drove them up on to a haymow in a barn.

"We sometimes ran away from school; two of us would go out at a time, so as not to throw any suspicion on the gang. Our rules were that all members should be present Wednesdays and Saturdays, and each boy should pay equal parts for ball. When there were disputes the officers would most always settle them."

The Tennis Club

This is a thoroughly good gang, one of the best gangs I know. In fact, I came to know about it at all only because one of its members dropped out, joined the distinctly evil "Dowser Glums," the account of which immediately follows that of the Tennis Club, and as a result got himself into various kinds of trouble. The same boy gave me the stories of the two gangs, adding frankly, "If I had stopped in the Tennis Club, I should never have been sent to a Reform School." A thoroughly worthless man, twenty-six years old, was in the Glums, while Mr. M., the father of one of the boys, was practically in the Tennis Club. The contrast cannot be described in words.

There were fifteen boys in the Tennis Club, twelve to seventeen years of age, all Americans except two Swedes.

"Met at tennis court at M.'s house. Met after school, nights and Saturdays. Had a captain of baseball nine, captain of football, and treasurer. Treasurer collected things at M.'s house,—gloves, rackets, etc. If a fellow was a good ball player or an all-round athlete, let him in. Sometimes fellows [by way of initiation] pounce on a fellow and give it to him for two or three minutes. Tell a fellow he didn't belong there and he would leave. Been going together for seven months when I left off going.

"M.'s parents would buy things for their boy and we could use them. We played tennis, baseball, football, cricket; went bicycle riding; camping out. Went a little ways from M.'s house; went out to camp days, swimming, boating. Made a boat and went fishing for pickerel and perch. Play ball and cricket after supper till dark. Sit in porch and talk over stories a little after dark.

"Ring doorbells and play tick-tack on windows of fellows of our club. Sometimes would have a fight; other fellows would stop it. Never let a big fellow pick on a little fellow. We were against smoking."

The Dowser Glums

This tough gang contained four Irish boys, three French, one American. The members were for the most part seventeen or eighteen years of age, except the man of twenty-six. The place-names, I suppress, as of no interest.

"Met out in the woods back of an old barn on Spring Street. Met every day if we did not get work. Any fellow could bring in a fellow if others approved. Put a fellow out for spying or telling anything about the club. Tell him we didn't want him and then if he didn't take the hint force him out. It had been going for two years; broke up now, I think.

"We played ball; went swimming, fishing, and shooting. Each of us had a rifle. Meet [at night] and tell stories of what we had done during the day. Go to shows. Go and watch dancing class. Sundays we loafed around streets. Sometimes went on a trip in the country. Went shooting. Other days catch a freight and go to W—— and L——. Went to B—— to shows and circus.

"Purpose of club was to steal; most anything they could get their hands on; fruit off from fruit stands; snag ice-cream at picnics. Robbed a store and put it in an old barn,—revolvers, knives, and cartridges. Work for two or three days, then loaf round and spend our money; spend money for circus. Sometimes folks would make us spend for clothes. Play cards,—poker, whist, high low jack. Played in the woods. Smoke cigarettes, pipe, and cigars. Biggest fellow drank; he tried to make the other fellows drink but they wouldn't."

The Island Gang

Twelve boys: four Irish, three French, two Poles, two Germans, one Jew. Ages between twelve and eighteen, but generally about fifteen. The boy who told me the story, one of the Frenchmen, said with much pride, "We never got caught stealing." I have since watched boys stealing from the big markets; they certainly have reduced it to a science!

"Met on L. Street; all lived on that street. Would not let any gang on that street. Give a strange boy a licking.

"M. was ring-leader,—steals most; says, 'Come on'; biggest and oldest. Didn't let anybody in after we started; been going together five years. M. started it, and asked us to be in the gang.

"We played run-sheep-run, tag, relievo, hide and seek. Stay out all night; have a fire down by the foundry. Go to shows Monday and Saturday nights; like Railroad Jack, Great White Diamond, White Eagle; like plays where there was fighting.

BOYS "JUMP FREIGHTS" BECAUSE THEY "LIKE TO GO AND SEE PLACES"

"WE FOUGHT FOR THE FUN OF IT"

"Jumped freights to S— — and P— —. Ran away from home to U— —; stayed up there two weeks. Hated to go to school; ran away because I didn't like to study. Saw boys out, so I liked to stay out and play baseball. Go to W— — Market in a crowd; steal apples, candy, grapes, and peanuts; we never got caught.

"Put wires across the sidewalks. Fight with another gang; fought for the fun of it, to see which was the strongest; fought with clubs. If there was a dispute in our crowd, leader settled it. If two fellows were fighting for a thing, the leader took it away from them and gave it to another fellow. If a member of the gang lied to one of us fellows, we called him a squealer; if he told on us, we called him a spy.

"Get our money from junk. Drink beer. All smoke. We had our best times bunking out, ringing doorbells, and tying cats' tails together. We like to plague girls,—ask them for a kiss, and things like that."

The Medford Street Gang

Six boys: two Americans, four Irish. Ages between twelve and fifteen. This is, paradoxically, a bad gang of good boys. Five out of the six members landed in Reform Schools, and I knew personally four of the five. All were distinctly above the average, and all are now doing well in life.

"Met on corner of street. We had three different leaders; I was leader; St. J. was leader. When we first moved there we gathered together and kept together all the time.

"We played baseball, football, cricket, tag, and hide and seek. We had a tent,—stayed out nights. We stole pigeons, broke into slot machines. We all divided up about the same. If a fellow lied to one of us, we put him out of the crowd for a week. Used to think school was too hard; didn't want to go because there was a show in town; stayed away just for the fun of it. Best time was going to theatre, like comical plays, Irishmen and fighting.

"We never used to think of girls, ["How do you treat them?" I had asked.] I don't know how to treat them; never tried it."

Another boy's report of the same Gang—one year later

The gang now contained seven boys: four American, three Irish.

"Met every day, right after school, corner Medford Street and Somerville Avenue; thought that Medford Street belonged to us. If a strange boy came around, try to pick up a fight with him to see if he was a good fighter. A. was leader; St. J. was leader sometimes. Anybody moved around there we thought safe to come in, would let him in. Put a fellow out if he go and tell on us. We have been going together five or six years.

"We play baseball, hoist the sail, how many miles to Barbery; go to beach; go to theatre once or twice a week, City Square and Grand Opera House; like love plays best. Sundays go around in city; wander around the streets; go to beach. Other days go down to freight yards and jump freights. We used to snowball Jews who came to slaughter house to get food. Plague a man down there; ring doorbells; play tick-tack. Steal money, candy, hens, iron, and fountain pens.

"All of us smoked. Get lager beer Saturday nights off beer wagons. Boys gamble with dice; shoot craps. Chuck a fellow out who made a dispute."

The Methuen Gang

Six boys: five Irish and one "Yankee," between thirteen and sixteen years of age. This is an especially adventurous gang, whose chief amusement is travel. Note especially the characteristic initiation to test the candidate's resourcefulness.

"I was called 'Bull-dog,' because I stuck to it when I started a thing. C. called 'Gulliver' because he traveled around so much. M. called 'Puggie' because he had a flat nose. O. was leader; biggest and best fighter.

"When one fellow went out, let another fellow in; get a fellow who would keep things to himself; make him take an oath. Put him [as initiation] on a freight train and send him off alone to see if he could get back alone; if he came back he was a member of the gang.

"Been going together three years. All live on the same street. Play baseball, football, punch bag, tag, hide and seek, bull in the ring, leap frog. Build forts and capture them.

"Go to boys' club twice a week. Go to shows two or three times a week. Like tragedies. Get up shows ourselves and let fellows from the district in. Went to a show and traveled with the show as far as W— —. Stay out all night sometimes. Go off to different cities. Jump freights. Sundays sometimes go off on a fishing trip, or a picnic out in the country.

"Plague the ragman; upset his cart; run off with the rags. Ran away with banana team. All work for a spell and then all loaf a while. If one of the gang got hit, stand up for one another. Save up our money and then go off for a good time; go to B— — Saturday afternoons; buy our tickets on that trip."

Boys' gangs, then, as one may readily infer from the foregoing accounts, are of various types. They may be large or small, good or bad, long-lived or evanescent. Yet with all their superficial differences, they are fundamentally alike. Each exists for the sake of a definite set of activities—to play games, to seek adventure, to go swimming, boating, and playing Indians in the woods, to make mischief, to steal, to fight other gangs. Few are the groups which do not, at one time or another, do all these things. Especially noteworthy is the desire of the gang for a local habitation—its own special street corner, its clubroom, its shanty in the woods.

All normal gangs, in short, are so much alike that if we discovered any group among the lower animals acting with equal uniformity, we should unhesitatingly ascribe their behavior to instinct. Without doubt, there is a gang-forming instinct set deep in the soul of boyhood. Whoever, therefore, would understand boys, must study their spontaneous organizations.

CHAPTER III

THE ORGANIZATION OF THE GANG

Age of members— Their habitat, nationality, and social class— Permanence of and definiteness of organization of gangs— Their names— Times and places of meeting — Officers— Initiation ceremonies— Rules— Resignations and expulsions— Method of settling disputes— Emergence of the group mind.

THE gang age, as we have seen, is from ten to sixteen. In a few cases, this organized group life begins as young as seven; in a few, also, it lasts up to eighteen or nineteen. Between thirteen and fourteen is the average age; and in a general way, the boy's social education in the gang takes about five years. Before this period, the little boy plays a good deal by himself, or plays in company with other boys a good deal as if he were playing alone. After it, he cultivates individual friendships, or courts a girl.

Nearly always, the gang is a strictly local affair, limited to a certain district or to one or two streets. "We all live on L street," run the boys' reports. "We all come from one street and a little street off from it." "Fellows who lived up that way could be in the crowd." "Come from down around the wharves." "If he lived down there, and the fellows knew him, he could get in with them." The neighborhood spirit is strong in boys; it needs to be regarded in all social work.

Nationality and Social Class

As for nationality, the gang is apt to be thoroughly unprejudiced and democratic. To be sure, twelve of my sixty-six gangs were all of one nationality. But that is largely because the streets or sections of the city where the boys live are likely to be given up to a single race. Fifty-four of my gangs were of mixed nationality, while in only one was any line drawn at breed or color—"No Jews or Negroes allowed." Far more than we realize, the boys' gang is helping out the public school in the great problem of assimilating the diverse races in the United States.

Nevertheless, there are some curious differences of nationality in the membership of gangs. Irish boys are especially gangy, with Americans and French a good second. Jews, on the other hand, are conspicuous for their absence. I questioned several Jewish boys, without discovering a single typical gang; and only two of my sixty-six gangs had Jewish members, though Jews are decidedly numerous in the regions from which the boys came. The reader who is interested in race psychology will find food for thought in the differing instincts of Irishman and Jew.

There is also some social difference in boys' gangs. Boys from well-to-do homes are, as one might expect, less gangy than those brought up amid poorer surroundings. In the case of the more fortunate boys, the gang is only one of a number of factors in their social development. But boys from bad, broken, or inefficient homes are forced to provide their own social life, and the gang is their one instinctive reaction to their social environment.

Curiously, too, boys from the better class of homes more often form their social groups *de novo* to suit their individual social needs; while boys whose home training is deficient tend more to become members of gangs already formed. For this reason the permanent and long-lived gangs are apt to be tough, with fixed and dangerous traditions. Thus, while among well brought up boys a gang rarely survives the boyhood of the group which formed it, among delinquents of my acquaintance hardly more than a quarter were original members of their gangs, or could tell how their gangs started. The bad gang, therefore, tends to be a persistent and dangerous institution, taking in new members as the older ones graduate. But the good gang dies young. This circumstance probably accounts in no small degree for the bad odor in which all boys' gangs are commonly held.

Organization

In respect to definiteness of organization, there are marked differences in gangs. Some are loosely knit and of short duration; others are select in their membership and rigid in their structure, so that they last through several generations of boys. Some gangs are autocratic, some democratic,—this, naturally, depending largely on the leader.

Most of them have names,—The Hicks Street Fellows, The Bleachery Gang, Morse Hollow Athletic Club, Wharf Rats, Crooks, Liners, Eggmen, Dowser Glums. Most have a regular time and place of meeting, rules and officers, though only a few have written constitutions and by-laws. Moreover, the definiteness of the organization and the *esprit de corps* seem to be quite independent of any formality or written code. Two organizations may be equally definite and forceful; and yet one may have its organization explicit in articles of federation, while that of the other is covert in the brain and muscles of its leader.

Time and Place of Meeting

Boys at the gang age intend to get together whenever possible. They will use all the time in which they are free from work or school. I have known boys to leave their proper occupations to go with the gang; and to reckon out carefully the balance between a day's fun with the gang and a general warming-up reception at night by father. Most of the sixty-six gangs met every day, many met morning, noon and night, or all day. The evening hours are, naturally, the most active and the most dangerous part of the day, for then mischief-making is likely to be rampant, encouraged under the veil of darkness.

During the larger part of the year in most parts of the United States boys prefer the outdoor life. In the cities, a certain street or corner is the customary meeting-place. In the fall and winter months boys look for shelter. In the country they build a cabin of boards or logs in the woods; in the city they get clubrooms, make a shanty in the back yard, or fix up an empty room in the cellar, attic, or shed. In one gang, for example, "the Club met down at one boy's house—in the cellar of the shed. Fixed up the place, had pictures out of magazines and papers,—funny pictures. Made a little table and benches, had boxing-gloves. Two boys had them an hour. No fighting allowed. Spent our evenings in the 'Clubroom.' Go to church Sundays and then skip down to the club and read books."

In general, about half the city gangs have their regular meeting-place on street or street corner. For the other half, my records show four gangs meeting in clubrooms; three in houses; two in a shed; and one each in a shanty, behind a barn in the woods, in a house made of old barrels in a back street, a hencoop, a hut in the woods, a tent in the woods, a tent in the yard, a dugout, an empty attic, and the cellar of a shed.

Boys do not like parlors. They prefer a rather rough and crude place in shed or attic which they can fix up to suit their own tastes. Benches, working-tools, boxing-gloves, punching-bags, pictures, magazines and books, form the natural furniture of a gang clubroom. Fortunate, indeed, are the parents who can provide the right kind of a room in their home for their boys, and are wise enough to let the neighbors' boys use it freely, without too much attention to their muddy feet.

Naturally, the boys have a sense of ownership of their clubroom tents or camps; but we find the same sentiment of ownership developing over the street or corner where they meet. The following are familiar expressions of the boys in regard to ownership: "Had a shanty in the woods. Other fellows would come and tear it down. Had a right over it." "Wouldn't let any gang in that street. Gave a strange boy a licking." "Thought that Medford Street belonged to us." "Every corner has a gang. That corner belongs to us."

Officers

Two boys said: "We didn't have no leader." This is not correct. Consciously or unconsciously there must be a leader in every social group. A few gangs have a long list of officers elected formally by ballot at stated periods. But forty-four gangs (66⅔ per cent) have one leader, who takes his position naturally with little form or ceremony. Of the sixty-six gangs—

1	gang had	six officers or leaders
1	gang had	four officers or leaders
4	gangs had	three officers or leaders
8	gangs had	two officers or leaders
44	gangs had	one officer or leader
8	gangs had	no regular leader

The following words express the spirit of the boys in reference to leadership:—

"J. was ringleader. Steals most; says, 'Come on.'" "I was leader. Had stumps, and the one who could do the most stumps would be leader." "D. was the leader. He could fight best and had most money." "G. was leader. He gave you anything if he had it. Worst one in the gang." "G. was leader. Big, strong fellow. He is always bringing a gang around him." "D. was leader. Pretty good fellow. Most daring fellow. Choose him by ballot. He got seven votes." "No regular leader. One fellow proposed a thing. He knew most about it, and take the lead."

The leader of the gang is such an interesting personality that we shall make a more careful study of him later, in another work.

Initiation

Commonly when boys enter a new gang some form of a reception is tendered them. In winter the new fellow may get a rub in the snow; in summer months he may be given a ducking or a little rough-and-tumble good time. In the Jenhine Boys, the new fellow "had to wrestle with Gibson to see if he was strong," while in the Tennis Club, they "pounce on a fellow and give it to him for two or three minutes." In a few gangs there were definitely planned initiation ceremonies. In the Jeffries Point Gang they threw a new fellow up in the air for five or ten minutes to test his grit. "If he didn't cry, let him in."

The object of the initiation ceremony appears to be to test the new fellow's grit and strengthen his spirit of loyalty.

Rules

In the sixty-six gangs we find—

18	rules as to	"squealing," snitching, or tell-taleing
8	rules as to	lying to one of the gang
8	rules as to	standing by each other in trouble
5	rules as to	"divvying up" or paying equal parts of the expenses
3	rules as to	unjust fighting
2	rules as to	using tobacco
1	rule as to	swearing
1	rule as to	stealing

We find the demand for loyalty and justice in the foreground and for morality in the rear. Although the rules are rarely put on paper there are few gangs without an unwritten code. These rules are necessary for the existence of the gang. They must be strictly enforced or the gang is dissolved. Expulsion is the usual penalty.

Dropping out of Gangs and Expulsion

Boys drop out of the gang suddenly, so that very few remain after sixteen years of age. At this time boys are entering the second adolescent period, and become intensely interested in girls. They feel so far above boys twelve or thirteen years old that they no longer care to affiliate with them. In gangs where younger boys have been allowed to enter, the older boys retire without disturbance to the structure of the group or its object; but in a gang where younger members have not been admitted and the boys are about the same age, the group may sometimes continue with a new set of interests.

As for involuntary withdrawals, ten boys were expelled from their gangs for "squealing," three for unjust fighting, one each for bossing, failure to pay dues, cowardice, getting fresh, and disobedience. "Kicked one fellow out," ran the reports, "for telling on the others." "Put a fellow out for fighting with another boy. The other fellow was in the right." "Put him out because he would run off when needed to fight."

Settling Disputes

Disputes are sure to arise in any social group and especially in a gang. "If there was any dispute, have a scrap over it. Fellow who got the worst of it, gave up." "If there was a dispute the leader settled it." "The officers would most always settle disputes, talk it over, get circumstances, and then settle it."

These cases illustrate the most common methods of settling internal troubles. In ten cases the boys fought it out; in seven other cases the matter was settled by the leader, a bigger boy, or an outsider.

The typical boys' gang, then, is no mere haphazard association. Accidents of various sorts—age, propinquity, likeness of interests—bring together a somewhat random group. Immediately the boys react on one another. One or more leaders come to the fore. The gang organizes itself, finds or makes its meeting-place, establishes its standards, begins to do things. It develops, in some sort, a collective mind, and acts as a unit to carry out complex schemes and activities which would hardly so much as enter the head of one boy alone. The gang is, in short, a little social organism, coherent, definite, efficient, with a life of its own which is beyond the sum of the lives of its several members. It is the earliest manifestation in man of that strange group-forming instinct, without which beehive and ant hill and human society would be alike impossible.

CHAPTER IV

CERTAIN ACTIVITIES OF THE GANG

Analysis of gang activities— Survivals from pre-gang stage— Group games— Tribal industries— Boys' reports of these— Their significance— "Plaguing people"— Boys' reports— Instinctive nature of the impulse— Stealing— Reports.

THE most active time of life is early adolescence. At this age, the normal boy has finished one stage in his development, and is resting before he enters upon the next. He has weathered the storms of childhood. He has completed some of the most difficult portions of the growth process, and has salted down his gains. Between eight years of age and twelve, lies a period of extraordinary toughness and resilience, when the boy can eat anything and do anything. He is simply one bundle of prodigious energy, which he must explode, and which he generally insists on exploding in his own way.

The gang, naturally, becomes the chief outlet for his activities. Sheldon, in his study of 851 boys who were members of gangs, found that the purposes of these spontaneous societies were:—

Athletics	61%
Migration, building, hunting, fighting, and preying	17
Industrial work	8½
Or to sum up, associations for purposes involving physical activity comprised	86½
While associations for social, secret and literary purposes comprised only	13½

My own more detailed study of sixty-six gangs reveals the following group activities:—

Group games,—baseball, football, basketball, hockey, etc.	53	gangs or	80%
Tribal industries,—hunting, fishing, boating, building huts, going about in the woods, playing Indians, etc.	49	gangs or	74
Predatory activities,—stealing, injuring property, etc.	49	gangs or	74
Fighting	46	gangs or	70

Swimming	45	gangs or	68
Migrations	44	gangs or	67
"Plaguing people"	44	gangs or	67
Going to theatres	38	gangs or	58
Running-games,—relievo, chase, tag, etc.	31	gangs or	47
Smoking	50	gangs or	45
Playing cards	25	gangs or	38
Skating	20	gangs or	50
Sliding	12	gangs or	18
Drinking	9	gangs or	11

Of these various group activities, the running-games belong properly to the pre-gang stage of the boy's existence. The normal instincts of the little boy incline him to the individualistic games, of which tag and hide and seek are the type, in which the player acts for himself against the one who is "it." The transition to the coöperative "group games" of the gang age not infrequently takes place by way of running-games of the prisoner's base and relievo type, in which, though the game is still fundamentally individualistic, there is nevertheless some sort of loosely organized side.

Running being a deep-seated impulse of all young life, the formless running-games of childhood tend to hold over into the gang age. Thirty-one of my sixty-six gangs, or practically half of them, reported that they still clung to their pre-adolescent sports. Tag, hide and seek, and relievo are the favorites, being represented in twenty-one, fourteen, and twelve gangs respectively. Hoist the sail, chase, leap frog, and run-sheep-run, appear in five gangs or more. Some twenty other games, a few of them apparently local inventions, are mentioned at least once. Oddly enough, some of the oldest stand-bys of childhood, such as puss in the corner, blind man's buff, and follow the leader, appear in but two gangs at most, while tops, marbles, and kites figure not at all. Only two gangs—more's the pity—play hare and hounds; partly, let us hope, because of the limitations imposed by the city streets rather than altogether because of deficient wind and stamina in the city-bred boy.

Of the group games—of games, that is, which presuppose an organized side, a leader, rules, apparatus, and some sort of playing-field—baseball, as might be expected, comes easily first. Fifty-one gangs play baseball, of the fifty-three which devote themselves to group games. Football comes next, with thirty-six. Hockey and basketball make a bad third and fourth, with nine each. Cricket appears in six gangs. If, then, we lump together the cricket-playing and baseball-playing gangs, as we may fairly do since they are both bat-and-ball games of essentially the same type and really alternates of one another, we arrive at the significant fact that all normal boys, at the age when they have the native impulse to form gangs, have also the native impulse to hit a quick-moving object with a club. The precise significance of this conjunction, and the part which it ought to play in the boy's education, will appear later.

Of swimming, also, and the minor sports of boyhood, of smoking and drinking and playing cards, I shall have more to say in another place. For the present we are concerned only with such activities as arise from the great fundamental instincts of the gang age.

Of these, next in importance to the group games come the so-called tribal industries,—hunting, fishing, building boats and rafts and sailing them, going to ponds or into the woods, building huts and playing Indians,—the various uncivilized occupations, in short, with which the savage tribes of the world fill the greater part of their lives.

On this point the most entertaining witnesses are the boys themselves. I quote, therefore, their own accounts.

"Played Indians in the woods. Went fishing after perch and pickerel. Went berrying. Got a pail full, then ate them." "Went fishing and shooting. Each of us had a gun. Played cards in the woods. Met out in the woods back of an old barn. Sundays, went on a trip into the country." "Went camping out. Stayed for a day or two. Made a boat. Went bathing, fishing for perch and pickerel." "Went fishing. Had a tent in the woods for one month. Went boating." "Went fishing. Went to woods on Sundays. Built bonfires. Went hunting." "Went fishing for pickerel and perch. Went hunting for gray squirrels, pheasants, quails, rabbits, foxes. Shot three foxes, one silver fox. Had a shanty in the woods." "Made boats and rafts to hold ten or twelve fellows. Twenty-three of us hired a tent for five days in woods." "Played Indians. Made up two parties. One party captured others and put them in a hole. Met in a shanty or clubhouse in the woods." "Had a tent and a dugout a quarter of a mile out in the woods. Stayed out five nights. Slept in a barn."

These are sample reports. In one form or another, three quarters of our boys' gangs find themselves impelled to revert to the conditions of pre-civilized days, and to enjoy what their savage forebears had perforce to endure. Considering that these gangs are nearly all made up of city boys, who have to put themselves to a great deal of trouble to get out into the country, the fact is most significant.

Closely allied to this instinctive liking for savagery is an instinct for "plaguing people." All proper boys have it, while nearly seventy per cent of the boys of this study report that making themselves collectively disagreeable is one of the spontaneous activities of their several groups. As before, I subjoin the boys' own account.

"Rap on doors. Push and pull people. Play tick-tack on windows." "Plague Jews and Italians. Tip the rag teams of Jews over. Take the rags and sell them to some other Jew." "Have a dead rat. Throw it at a Chinaman. Fire things at men to get the chase. Hit men out of doors to get the chase. Put a rock in a paper bag for men to kick." "Tie a rope across the street and trip people up. Throw eggs at people. Throw cabbages at people. Ring doorbells. Break windows, electric lights. Plague Chinamen. Bring them in a bundle of paper [to wash]. Throw potatoes at Chinamen." "Call persons names to get the chase. Throw eggs at Chinamen's doors. Plague policemen." "Go round in wood yard. Throw wood in street to get the chase."

A FOOT-BALL GAME BETWEEN CITY GANGS

The crosses indicate the leaders

"A SHANTY OR CLUB HOUSE IN THE WOODS"

So the records run,—pure, wanton, useless mischief and cruelty. No wonder the gang is not popular. Yet we all did the same things in our day and have grown up to be very decent men. There is a time in the lives of normal boys when any form of distress—to other people—is instinctively amusing. Note also how frequently the boy annoys simply "to get the chase." He has the hunting instinct; he has also the instinct for being hunted. Therefore he deliberately exasperates some adult beyond endurance, until the man "takes after" him, wrath in his eye and anticipation in the palm of his hand. The man, commonly, is the fleeter of foot; but the boy has the better wind and the advantage of a short start. As a last resort, he can dodge. The resulting game is, on the whole, the most thrilling experience of boyhood. Nine times in ten, the boy gets away; the penalties that follow being caught are a cheap price for the riotous delights of escaping with the skin of his teeth.

Somewhat allied to plaguing people is stealing. The stealing instinct is strong in boys, so that even the good country gangs, with all they want to eat at home, devote part of their time to their neighbors' orchards and vineyards. The impulse is closely connected with the instinct for property, and is so entirely normal at the gang age that the boy, otherwise of good character, who steals in company, is seldom at all depraved. The boy who goes off by himself to steal is a different case.

That the crime of larceny reaches its climax before the age of twenty-one, shows that the predatory instincts and habits are early formed, or else that if the stealing instincts and habits increase in power after this age, the person becomes shrewd enough in stealing to escape the penalty of the law. The following reports of the boys in regard to stealing are instructive:—

"Go around stealing for fun. Go out to [a town ten miles from the city] for apples, pears, and things. Steal off baker's team; take basket of doughnuts and pies. Take milk out of doorways. Take bananas off banana team. Steal clothes off of clothes lines; sell to ragman. Steal junk; sell it to another ragman." "Steal coal and wood. Build fires. Steal anything we could get hold of off of fruit stand. Steal wood off farmer's team coming into the city." "Hit a Sheeney. He drop his bag and another fellow take it." "Stole pigeons. Broke into slot machines. Get lager beer Saturday nights off beer teams."

The boys' own reports of their thefts sum up as follows:—

(1) Things to eat (apples, pears, cakes, pies, oranges, bananas, etc.)	198	different things
(2) Things to sell (lead, coal, wood)	23	different things
(3) Things used in games (balls, bats, gloves, etc.)	48	different things
(4) Tools (saws, hammers, knives)	36	different things
(5) Jewelry (watches, rings, etc.)	24	times
(6) Animals and birds (dogs and pigeons)	24	times
(7) Money	80	times
Total	433	things and times

There was no use in asking the boys how many times they had taken fruit; life would be too short to take down the answers.

CHAPTER V

FURTHER ACTIVITIES OF THE GANG

Migration— Reports— Truancy— Reports— Theatre-going— Reports— Fighting— Personal fights— Fights between groups inside the gang— Fights between gangs— A case of war between federations of gangs.

There is probably no more characteristic difference between boyhood and middle age than the strange *Wanderlust* of youth. We adults are content to work year after year at the same desk, and think ourselves lucky if we can warm our feet year after year over the same register. But the boy,—

"He must go, go, go away from here,"

and "the old spring fret comes o'er him" at all seasons of the year.

Migratory Activities

The migratory impulse takes a sudden rise at the dawn of adolescence. Nearly all boys with good, red blood in their veins are touched by it. It appears to come as a strong wave at the gang age, and then gradually subsides; but it rarely entirely disappears.

Boys in their gangs love to tell and to hear stories of adventure, and there is no question that the gang is often a direct agent for stirring the call of the wild. In forty-four (67 per cent) of the sixty-six gangs there are records of the travel of one or more of the group. A boy who has taken some adventurous trip is a hero, and his stories are listened to with great zest. Boys rarely go off in large companies, for it is impossible for them all to get away at once. Commonly, not more than three or four go at a time; often a boy and his companion together; sometimes a boy goes alone.

In the following records, I have, as before, suppressed such geographical names as would be meaningless to most readers, and substituted for them some suggestion of the distance, or indicated whether the journey was from country to city, or the reverse.

"From A—— [a city of 100,000 people] go to B—— [a neighboring town] Sunday afternoons. Jump freights other days and go to [two other large cities, one of them nearly a hundred miles away]. Stayed out one or two nights. Ran away from home [nearly two hundred miles]. Stayed there two weeks."

"Sometimes go on a trip in the country on Sundays. Catch a freight, go to [near-by towns]. Go to B—— to shows and circus."

"Take a car, go to City Point, just for a little ride. Nice and breezy on the cars. Went to C—— on a freight. Got back same night about one o'clock. Go off for a trip on Sundays. Go out to A——, W——. Went to P—— [one hundred miles]. Had a tent in the woods for a month."

"Jumped freights. Was going to New York. Stopped [on the way]. Went back, was arrested."

"Took walks to Y—— Woods and R——'s Pond. Some saved up money and went to L—— Fair [one hundred and thirty miles each way]. Some went to [state capital] to ball-games."

"Broke into a store and then ran away from home so we wouldn't get caught. Went to B—— on a freight. Stayed at Hawkins Street Home one night. Went to O—— on freight. Stopped for a week in Armory in O——. Walked to N—— [ten miles] to sister's. Stayed a couple of days. Went to W—— and then back to M——, and was caught. We planned to go to A—— [which would have taken them two hundred miles into three states]."

"Go off to different cities on freights. Went to P—— [one hundred miles], five or six times. Stayed a week once. Went to N—— twice. Stopped one day each time. Went to A—— six times. Stayed two weeks. Went to E—— five or six times [these are within fifty miles of home], stopped three or four days. Went [across into Canada three hundred and fifty miles]. Got a job in a steam laundry there. Saved up money and then went off for a good time."

"Stay out nights three months to a time. Stay in cellars, freight cars, and entries. Sundays go out to [a surburban town] to get apples and pears. Jump freights to R—— and K——. Get off and come right back."

"Stay out nights. Go in back yards and sleep. Run away to [nearest large city]. Walked. Took four days. Got arrested there."

"Go down to Apple Island in a boat. Stay out at night; stay in paper offices on Washington Street. Lots of boys get there at one and two o'clock for their papers. When woke up, say: 'I am waiting for the papers.' Run away from home several times. Get as far as W——, turn round and come back at nights. Say we would try it some other times."

Or, to sum up:—

23	boys had jumped freights to other towns or cities.
3	boys had walked to distant towns or cities.
4	boys had paid fares on cars to different towns or cities.
30	boys had gone off to distant cities.
14	of the thirty had run away from home.
16	had stayed out nights.

In addition to the records of travel found in these gangs, the following records taken later are interesting:—

Boy Number 1

L. E. has a fair home ten miles from Boston; both parents are living. This boy was fourteen years of age by the time he was finally committed to a Reform School and had run away from home eight times. He went the first time when eleven years old. His reason for going always was: "I like to see places." The places were, however, all near-by.

Trip A. "Went to F—— to the military encampment; stayed there two days. Walked to B—— [twenty miles] and stopped around the wharves. Begged something to eat. Slept in alleyways and in mission. Policemen caught me; took me to the station till father came and got me."

Trip B. "Went to R—— to watch them drive cows to get killed. Stopped there for three days and worked for something to eat by driving cows. Slept in the stock-yard barn."

Trip C. "Went to W—— to see them make guns and stopped at Arsenal two days. Went to C—— to a boy's house that I knew. Went to theatre, stopped out too late; policeman took me; father came and got me."

Trip D. "Went to H—— to the place where they keep warships. Stayed there a week looking at guns and things. Went on errands for men; slept in a barn; took some apples off a fruit stand; policeman took me; father came and got me."

Trip E. "Went to B—— again; liked to go to places. Went out for a week, catching fish [salt water fishing]; went out as far as a lighthouse; slept in a bunk. After return stayed in B—— four days. Went to R—— again to see them kill cows. Policeman took me; father came and got me."

Boy Number 2

"G. stole some money, $75, and asked me to go with him to see the world. 'We'll go to St. Louis, earn some change and come back.' Went to P—— from B——; stayed there two nights; went by boat to New York; and then, the same day, took boat to Norfolk, Virginia; stayed there three weeks. Went around taking in the theatres, concert gardens, and having a good time. Went to cut-rate office for a ticket to St. Louis; found it would take all our money. We went over to Baltimore, and then to Philadelphia. We were 'financially embarrassed.' Worked at a restaurant for something to eat. Struck Wanamaker's for a job. I got $4 a week. I told a hard-up story to the floorwalker and he gave me $1 in advance; hired a room for $1 a week. He [G., the chum] didn't pay anything toward the room, and bummed around looking for a job. We stayed in Philadelphia five weeks. I paid rent and meals for all but once. Man paid me off and gave me $2 extra. We told hard-up story to our landlady; she went and told the Associated Charities; two policemen came and took us. We would not tell right names; we were sent to the House of Detention for two weeks; sent me back to B—— and kept my chum. Sent me over to jail on C—— Street for three weeks. I would not tell my name; got bread and water twice a day. I told them that I lived on Cherry Street, New York. I was getting sick with the itch, and got scared, and told my right name. Folks didn't want to send me here; judge did it."

This was a boy of fine ability and not a bad fellow. You can see in his story noble traits of character. He stood by his chum and fed him; he had good grit. One does not like to think what might have become of him if he had not caught the itch.

Boy Number 3

"Father takes his money and Mr. D.'s up to the car barn. Mr. D. gave me the money [$27] to take to my father. Instead of going to my father, I jumped fence and went down to the city. I was going to New York. I bought a ticket, got on board of the special train, and went to New York. It was night. I slept at the station. Had some money left; went out and bought a telescope and other things I did not need. Went back and slept in the same station. Police officer took me and put me on the train. Mother would give me a flogging every time I came home. Father used to read newspapers how boys ran away and men escaped punishment. The day I went he read about a man who got shot in New York; another man shot him in the back of the head; when he was shot, he fell back and pulled the reins so the horse stopped; the other man got in and drove off; took man's money and dropped him with a stone in the river. After a while he floated, and murderer was caught in New Jersey."

Of course, it's a serious matter, this *Wanderlust* of boyhood, and the boy who indulges it often comes to irreparable harm. But, after all, what is there like this going to and fro in the world to teach self-reliance and a knowledge of men? All normal boys want to run away; it is rather to their credit when they remain at home.

Truancy

Truancy is another manifestation of the *Wanderlust*. It takes the combined restraint of good parents and good teachers to hold a boy in that public prison, a quiet schoolroom, in the brisk days of fall when the chestnuts are falling, or in the mild days of spring, when the birds return and the buds are bursting. Notice the very suggestive words of the boys in reference to school. The following answers came from different truants in answer to the question, "Why did you run away from school?"

"Miss P. [his teacher] was all right. When I could not get my lessons, she would not scold me, but helped me out on them. Miss L. [another teacher] had it in for me. I was to blame part of the time, but she blamed other folks' actions on me, and the school was right near the park. I could see them playing and having fun. I wanted to have some fun, too, so I ran away with another fellow."

"Run just to get away from school. Gather up old barrels and junk to get money to go to shows; used to go alone mostly."

"Liked all the teachers but one; she didn't like colored boys. I liked to walk around the streets and look into the big store windows. Ran away to go to the theatre, and to go to ride on the express wagon."

"I didn't like school; I didn't like geography and history. I liked to go to shows. Rather be out working than going to school. Went down around markets to get jobs; about four of us used to go together."

"Didn't like to be in there sitting down."

"Didn't like to study."

"Have to sit quiet as can be all day."

"Went to wharves to see them take out fish."

"Ran away to go swimming and nutting."

"Ran to go to the circus."

"Ran to go to the ball games."

"Ran to go fishing."

"No fun in school."

"Ran to go to theatre."

In short, the boy is a natural vagabond. He wants above all things excitement, experience, and adventure. He is not lazy, but he will do anything sooner than work steadily at desk or bench.

The Theatre

Such adventure as the boy cannot get at first-hand by running away from home, he gets at second-hand by way of the theatre. Boys have a raging passion for entertainments, and the stage gives them an opportunity to get much of life condensed into a deglutible form. Boys will do anything to get into the theatre,—pick over the dump, work hard, be good for a whole week,—all from a desire to learn something more about the world and to have a new experience.

Not many of us adults fully realize the power of the theatre in the lives of children in our cities and larger towns. According to a study made at Worcester, Massachusetts, of children between ten years of age and fourteen, it appears that one quarter never attend the theatre at all, another quarter go at least as often as once a month, while no less than half of all the children examined go habitually once a week or more frequently. There is no reason for supposing that Worcester is in any respect exceptional in this regard.

Let us note the reports of the boys themselves:—

"Go to shows two or three times a week; liked tragedies; get up shows and let fellows from our district come in."

"Go once or twice a week to the theatre; go to Bowdoin Square and Grand Opera; like love plays best."

"Go to shows once a week; Bowdoin Square, Grand Opera, Lyceum and Howard; like funny plays best. Father gives me money to go."

"Go to shows about every night; stay around and they would let us in late; hook our way in sometimes; jump over the banister when man's back was turned. Like to see men get shot; like to see trains come on the stage."

"Like tragedy best, where there was a hero in it. In the 'Devil's Island,' the hero was a fellow in the English army. One fellow was maltreated and sentenced to Devil's Island, but finally came out the victor."

"Like war plays. Liked the acting where there was fighting and singing. Ran away from school to pick coal to make some money to go to theatre."

"I like murders and plays that have villains in them. Got passes from fellows who go out after the first act."

"Saturday night go to theatre; like tragic plays best, where the hero kills the villain."

"Go to shows Saturday afternoons; like all kinds. I like war shows and heroes and all like that."

"We had the best time going to theatres; like comical plays; like to see Irishmen and fighting."

"Like plays with fighting in them best."

"Like hero plays."

"Like excitement and Indian plays best."

There were eleven different reports in regard to plays which boys liked. Uncle Tom's Cabin is mentioned in five of them. Others, mentioned once or twice, are Great White Diamond, Queen of the White Slaves, Steeple Chase, Railroad Jack, White Eagle, Devil's Island, Peggy from Paris, Girls from England, Under Southern Skies, Arnold the Traitor, Wedded in the Streets, Shaumus O'Brien, Limited Mail, The Power of the Cross, Paul Revere's Ride, New York Day by Day, American Gentleman, Heart of Maryland, Why Women Sin, Mrs. Wiggs of the Cabbage Patch, Across the Rockies, Younger Brothers, Night before Christmas, Monte Cristo, Midnight in Chinatown, Rip Van Winkle, James Brothers in Missouri, Eight Bells, Across the Pacific, Way down East, McFadden's Flats, The Blue and the Gray, Winchester.

The significant thing about these reports is the catholicity of the boys' taste. When there is no bad and demoralizing play to be seen, they are entirely willing to attend a wholesome and elevating one.

Fighting

A very common and annoying form of activity of gang boys is fighting. The struggle for existence has, until very recent times, tended to select the men of a tribe who were the best fighters. So the boys come naturally by the fighting instinct. All grown-up persons feel that fighting should not be allowed in their presence, and at the same time, that it would have been far better for the boys if they had not appeared on the scene at that critical moment. Boys will fight to maintain personal rights, to defend their honor, to settle disputes, to defend the camp ground. The very slightest offense will arouse their combative instinct. In fact, they enjoy fighting so much that if they have no proper reason for a fight, they will guy or throw stones at another gang to furnish them a sufficient cause for battle. One gang went so far as to arrange yearly a battle for the seventeenth of June.

In forty-six gangs (78 per cent) we find records of fighting of four different kinds:—

1. Personal fighting.
2. Group fighting inside of gangs.
3. Fighting between gangs.
4. Fighting between groups of gangs.

Personal Fights

"Fight if any one swore about my mother." "One fellow thinks he can lick the other fellows. They think he can't, so they start a scrap." "Have fights among ourselves. Put two fellows together for a fight." "A fellow wouldn't share up, so we fought him." "Fight about calling names."

Every boy has his code of honor. There are certain names which a boy will not allow himself to be called without a fight. Boys are very sensitive about names which cause disgrace to their mothers. I am not so sure but that every boy should have a code of honor which may not be disregarded in his presence.

Group fighting inside of gangs

"Used to make forts in fields and have fights between ourselves." "Had fights among ourselves over out and not out" [in baseball]. "Fight among ourselves over ball games."

There are six records of these internal group fights. In winter boys make forts and choose sides to fight over the capturing of these forts. These fights are usually good-natured but very hotly contested. In the many different disputes which must naturally arise in the group games, the side which is being imposed upon must stand for its rights and fight for them if necessary.

Fights between gangs

"Fought with another gang to see which was strongest. Fought with clubs." "Our gang from our school fought a gang from another school. Fought with sticks and stones. Chase fellows in streets. Split fellows' heads open." "Fought with High Street and Water Street gang if they touched one of our gang. Fought with fists." "Had a regular battle with Sewall Street gang. Made a fort on a hill. Sewall Street gang tried to take fort on us. We pelted them with snow balls. They took it once at seven o'clock while we were eating breakfast. We drove them out over a fence."

Gang fights are very common. The following explanations were given for them: "For the fun of it." "For the possession of a certain street." "For the possession of a fort." "The other gang squealed on them over tearing down a shanty." "Touched one of our fellows." "Plagued my brother." "Picked up a fight by throwing stones." "Arranged for a fight on the seventeenth of June."

A fight between gangs is often a desperate and sometimes a dangerous affair. It is a fight to a finish; and it calls for the highest kind of courage, loyalty, and self-sacrifice. A small boy often has to fight a large boy on the opposite side, and to hold his undivided attention while the fortunes of war are being settled on another part of the field of battle. In a single-handed fight a boy will acknowledge personal defeat; but in a gang fight, never until the whole gang is worsted. After a group victory, the boys enjoy talking it over, and the little heroes receive high praise from their larger comrades.

A Fight between Federations of Gangs

"C—— gang fought with E—— gang. Everybody thought the E—— fellows were picking on the little fellows too much. We had it all arranged right, but there was a traitor in our gang. He told the E——s. We met in the middle of the ice on M—— River. Fought with clubs, sticks, and stones. There were about four hundred of our boys and about the same number on their side. We licked. One of our fellows got knocked out. Half of us got it on the arms. The ice broke in on the river and a lot of our fellows pulled the other fellows out. We did not like to see them drown. One little fellow on the other side got drowned. In close quarters where we could not use our clubs, we used our fists."

This story reads like a fairy tale, but it is not. The battle was fought to protect the small boys of C——, as noble a principle in the boys as "Taxation without Representation" was to our fathers.

There is a great difference of opinion in regard to the pedagogical value of fighting. Many trainers of boys think that a fight is bad and should be universally condemned. But there appears to be no road to self-respect and social independence except for the youth to fight for his rights. The boy who refuses to fight, and runs away when he is being imposed upon, feels himself a coward. He loses respect for himself and the respect of his playmates. Non-resistance is, without dispute, an ideal for mature manhood, but there is grave danger of forcing standards of grown-up people on youths. More of interest in regard to boys' fighting will appear in a later study of the boy leader.

CHAPTER VI

THE ANTHROPOLOGY AND PSYCHOLOGY OF THE GANG

Certain human instincts— Differing instincts of boys and girls— Many instincts of boyhood are survivals from savagery— The Recapitulation Theory, therefore, the key to boy psychology— Not, however, a complete explanation— Certain qualities of the young look toward the future— Illustrations of these— Ancestral qualities persist when useful— Examples from instincts of both boys and girls.

It is not easy to realize that it was only a single generation ago when we used to think that the animals are ruled by instinct, man by reason. We know better now. What was once the "new" psychology has taught us that man has more separate instincts than any other creature that breathes, and that however superior his rational life, it is still based upon a substructure of primitive instincts which he shares with the beasts of the field.

The newborn infant feels on his skin the air of a cold world, and sucks in his first breath without knowing how or why. He manages, the first time he tries, about as well as he ever will, the decidedly complex operation of taking breath and food at the same time, crossing the two streams in his throat, and sending each to its proper destination without confusion with the other. When the proper time comes, the child who has gone on all fours like an animal gets up on his hind legs to walk like a man.

We are all of us, therefore, man and animals alike, born with the particular set of instincts which prompt us, without our taking thought, to whatever acts are essential to our physical life. Some of these instincts are active at birth; more lie dormant, to ripen and manifest themselves only at the proper age, each in its proper time. The impulse to walk and to utter words comes suddenly, in babyhood. The mating instincts appear only toward the end of adolescence. Metchnikoff will have it that at the end of a well-spent life, an instinctive longing for death replaces the will to live.

The physical differences between boys and girls are strikingly correlated with a difference in instinctive interests. Brought up alike, in a hundred little ways they are dissimilar. I have seen at a children's party, on the advent of a baby, every little girl leave the supper table to surround the new-comer, while every little boy kept on with his meal. Where the girl plays with dolls, the boy plays with bats and balls.

Among other divergences, the boy forms gangs. Girls do not form gangs. They belong to sets, and sets and gangs are quite different institutions. The set is exclusive, undemocratic. It has no organization, leaders, history, and it owns no property. The set snubs its rivals; the gang fights them. The members of a set also snub one another, quarrel, and backbite. There is none of the deep-seated, instinctive loyalty which the members of a gang have for each other. The normal boy may fight his friend; he does not "get mad at" him.

All this is only one aspect of the deep-seated difference between "the only two kinds of people there are in the world, men and women." Barring dolls and the ability to hurl missiles, little girls and little boys, as they emerge from babyhood, are not so very unlike. But somewhere about the age of ten, the little boy begins to undergo a transformation, which in the girl never takes place at all. He begins to develop the gang-forming instinct. He begins to want to do things which he cannot do at all alone; and cannot, moreover, do with any real satisfaction except in conjunction with a special group of his fellows. The once friendly boy becomes shy of adults, so that only the rare man or woman can retain his full confidence. Girls he scorns. His games tend now to be of the coöperative type, in which there is a definitely organized side, with a leader and more or less specialized functions among the players, and where one side wins or loses to the other as a whole. It is no longer each for himself, but each for the team. A girl can be taught to like this kind of game; a boy takes to it like a duck to water.

Apparently, then, a boy joins a gang and a girl does not for precisely the same reason that he throws stones while his sister tends lovingly the dolls that are beneath his contempt. Each is doing instinctively, as a child, for play, what grown men and women have been doing these thousand years for work.

For obviously the instinctive activities of the boys' gang are the necessary duties of the savage man. The civilized boy hunts, fishes, fights, builds huts in the woods, stands loyally by his fellows, and treats all outsiders with suspicion or cruelty, and in general lives the life and thinks the thoughts of the savage man. He is, for the moment, a savage; and he instinctively "plays Indians" as the real savage lives them.

General opinion has it that the boy instinctively plays Indians and follows the so-called tribal occupations as the direct result of his inheritance from some thousands of generations of savage ancestors who, willy nilly, have been doing these things all their lives. We commonly believe that the normal boy is possessed to throw stones at every moving object because his forebears got their livings or preserved their lives by throwing all sorts of missiles at prey and enemies, so that the fascination of sticks and clubs is but the reverberation of the not so very far off days when sticks and clubs were man's only weapons.

According to this doctrine, such a game as baseball is an epitome of man's prehistoric activities. To throw accurately and to run swiftly, to hit a quick-moving object with a club, is to revive, symbolically, the most absorbing of ancestral activities and the most vivid of ancestral memories. As the girl, tending her doll, is recapitulating the experiences of a hundred thousand mothers before her, so the boy, in the varied activities of his gang, is reproducing the life of long departed clans and tribes. The instinctive interests of both boys and girls are the result of the experiences of their ancestors.

All this, one need not point out, is the familiar recapitulation theory, the doctrine, that is to say, that the young of each species, our own included, tends to reproduce in the course of its youth the successive stages in the history of its ancestors. We are by turns invertebrates, gill-breathing vertebrates, lung-breathing vertebrates (we make the great change at birth), little monkeys, little savages, and finally civilized men and women.

It is an illuminating theory, and one, moreover, which goes far toward explaining many aspects of our human nature which without it would be largely meaningless. Especially is it the key to the behavior of boys at the gang age. The normal boy between ten and sixteen is really living through the historic period which, for the races of northern Europe, began somewhere this side of the glacial period, and came to an end with, let us say, the early middle ages. He is, therefore, essentially a savage, with the interests of a savage, the body of a savage, and to no small extent, the soul of one. He thinks and feels like a savage; he has the savage virtues and the savage vices; and the gang is his tribe.

Yet while nothing can be more evident than that certain characteristics of growing boys and girls, both physical and mental, are the result of a direct inheritance from the past, it is equally evident that certain others are not. In certain conspicuous traits, our children favor their long-departed ancestors; but in certain others they are even less like them than we. Our anthropoid ancestry were hairy; children are less hairy than adults. We have larger brains and shorter arms than our forebears, but our children have still larger brains, relatively, and still shorter arms than we. In a dozen different ways, the older a man grows, the more, not the less, apelike does he become; as, for example, in the curve of his back and the great bony ridges over his eyes. In these respects, the child looks rather to the future than to the past. The child, indeed, recapitulates the history of the race, but only so far as it is some real advantage to him to do so, and never merely for the sake of recapitulating. When Nature cannot utilize an ancestral quality here and now, out it goes, to make room for something wholly new.

Certain qualities of youth, then, are an inheritance from the past; they exist because of the men and women that were. Certain others are a prophecy of adult life, and exist because of the men and women who are to be. Most of our youthful characteristics are simultaneously of both these sorts. They have persisted from an immemorial past; but they have persisted, instead of being lost by the way, because they have proved themselves useful in this present. Thus, for example, we recapitulate a gill-slit stage, because we actually did have a fish ancestor; but we use these gill-slits, not to become adult fish, but as a convenient device for building an aortic arch such as no fish ever had. We are tailed embryos as a step in becoming tailless men; and in the same way, we are boy savages as a stage toward becoming civilized human beings. The savage impulses of a long departed past appear in every modern boy, both because they are an inheritance from that past and because they are a preparation for the boy's future. We tend to recapitulate only so much of the ancestral experience as we can actually use.

Conversely, what we keep is useful; or else has been useful so very lately that we have not had time to change. Before the days of gunpowder—and how short a while, after all, that was—handling spear and javelin was a matter of life and death. Then, as now, boys had the missile-throwing instinct, and girls did not. They had it, on the one hand, because their ancestors had been spear-men; but they had it, on the other hand, and equally, and long before they were old enough to fight, in order that they might enjoy the long continued practice that taught them to throw well. Evidently, a spear-fighting people whose boys lacked the throwing instinct, so that they had to be coerced into doing their spear practice, would soon go down before a rival group whose boys found spear throwing a spontaneous play. In the same way, the children of girls who did not love dolls and pets and all small and helpless things could never, even under modern conditions, make head against the children of girls who did. All the peoples whose women tended their babies from a sense of duty have long ago gone to the wall.

The woman must tend her babies; therefore the girl loves dolls. The man, to be a member of any human society, whether civilized or savage, must stand by his fellows, follow his leader, act with his associates, be loyal to the death. Therefore the boy has the gang-forming instincts. These are, in a real sense, an inheritance from the past, but they are in an equally real sense a gift of the present to the future. Boys and girls alike repeat so much of their common ancestral experience as helps to make them efficient men and women, and no more. If there were no such thing as heredity, if each generation simply sat down and created the next to suit itself, we should still have to make the girls love dolls and the boys form gangs. Without these instincts, neither girls nor boys would become fully equipped adults.

CHAPTER VII

THE CONTROL OF THE MORE PRIMITIVE IMPULSES

Certain maladjustments of human instincts to civilized life— These especially noteworthy in boyhood— Instinctive basis of cruelty in boys— Other causes of cruelty— Psychology of "plaguing people"— Pedagogic worthlessness of the impulse— Its cure— Impulse to plague girls of a different nature— Apparently protective— The love of fighting— Its instinctive nature— Fighting is, on the whole, a virtue— Its pedagogic value— Practical treatment of the problem— Two working rules— Self-limiting nature of the evil.

We must, then, so far as we are good evolutionists, look upon the boy's gang as the result of a group of instincts inherited from a distant past. So far as, in addition, we are good Darwinians, we must suppose that these gang instincts arose in the first place because they were useful once, and that they have been preserved to the present day because they are, on the whole, useful still.

Fortunately or unfortunately, however, the social evolution of *Homo Europeus* during, let us say, the last three or four centuries, has been vastly more rapid than any strictly biological evolution can possibly be. Inevitably, therefore, the bodily structure of man and his equipment of natural instincts, has of late years tended to fall behind the demands of civilization. Witness, for example, the professional man who falls in love at twenty, but must wait till thirty before he can support a wife; or the inconvenient superfluity of bone, muscle and lung in many an office worker. One notes incidentally how much better fitted for civilization, both in mind and body, women are than men. They were, the ethnologists tell us, civilized first.

Certain of the gang instincts, therefore, tend to fit the growing boy for conditions which no longer obtain, rather than for those which he will actually have to face as a man. To no small extent, the ancient virtues of savagery have become vices of civilization, so that the instincts on which they are based are by no means desirable in a modern boy.

Consider, for example, the "plaguing people" which, as we have seen, occurs in forty-four of our sixty-six reports. This is, of course, sheer savagery. "Most savages," as Darwin says, "are utterly indifferent to the sufferings of strangers, or even delight in witnessing them"; and the modern boy does not fall far behind the ancient savage as every Chinaman and Jew and policeman can testify. The gang considers it the proper thing also to attack and misuse every strange boy who appears in its precincts. It gets no small part of its pleasure in giving displeasure to others.

Yet, after all, the cruelty of our savage forefathers was a hard necessity. A little tribe, perpetually fighting for its life against its rivals, could not afford to be sympathetic toward the discomfort of outsiders. In the primitive struggle for existence, the kindly tribe would pretty certainly be beaten by the cruel one.

So the boy is cruel and plagues people. But his cruelty is largely collective rather than individual, like that of the wolf rather than the tiger. As his ganginess fades with later adolescence, much of his native barbarity will go with it. Till that time comes, the wise adult will not attribute to thoroughgoing depravity what is only a temporary stage in the boy's psychic evolution.

In part, therefore, the boy comes honestly by his teasing instincts. But "plaguing people" arises in part also from race prejudice; and so far as it does thus arise, it is entirely the fault of us adults. Boys, untaught, have no prejudice against any particular kind of stranger, so that the fault being ours, the remedy is quite in our own hands.

To a large extent, moreover, the practice of being disagreeable is, as the boys themselves report, merely "to get the chase." "Plaguing people" is an exciting sport, which satisfies a natural thirst for adventure, and which is therefore most naturally controlled by judicious doses of adventure in other forms. The joy of getting the chase necessarily departs as soon as the running instincts begin to fade, and the growing boy begins to encounter the gang's prejudice against fleeing from a pursuer not much stronger than himself.

Still, for the most part, this inconvenient impulse of boyhood is largely a spontaneous instinct, allied to the disposition to tease and bully. It is doubtful if it has any pedagogical value whatever. Its proper cure is in about equal measure, firm repression and a cultivation of the sympathetic imagination. But let the parent beware of cultivating a sympathy which is in the least sentimental. It is better to let the boy stay naturally cruel for a few years, and then as naturally outgrow it, than to make him morbidly philanthropic for life. After all, cruelty, however hard on the victim, so long as it is unconscious, does little moral damage to the perpetrator.

The tendency to plague the girls, however, seems to be an instinct of a different sort. In general, boys at the gang age do not naturally associate with girls, do not allow them in their organizations, nor have any interests in common with them. In fact, boys seem to be impelled by a well defined impulse to make themselves disagreeable to the other sex.

Only eleven of my reports so much as recognize the existence of the beings who, five years later, will become the most absorbing objects in life; while even in these, the information came only on inquiry, not spontaneously. To the question: "How does your gang treat girls?" typical answers are: "We never used to think of girls. I don't know how to treat them. I never tried it." "We never used to go with any girls." "They never go round with any girls. They never say nothing to them.

Sis at them." "Sometimes do mean things to them. Swear at them. Fight them. Steal things off them. Call them names."

Who can question that this instinctive hostility of boys to girls is a wise provision of nature, and a good thing—at least for the boys? It is a temporary stage which passes all too soon, and leaves the youth at the mercy of the first attractive girl who makes the sweet eyes at him. From ten years to sixteen, nature tries to keep the sexes apart; presumably she knows what she is about, and we shall do well to accept the hint which she offers us.

Closely allied to plaguing, and even more nearly universal in normal gangs, is fighting. Unlike plaguing, however, fighting is on the whole a virtue of the gang rather than a vice, notwithstanding its many regrettable aspects. Boys enjoy fighting, and they ought to. We come of a stock which has fought its way up from barbarism, and has known the joy of battle these hundred centuries. "We, the lineal representatives of the successful enactors of one scene of slaughter after another, must, whatever more pacific virtues we may also possess, still carry about with us, ready at any moment to burst into flame, the smouldering and sinister traits of character by which they lived through so many massacres, harming others, but themselves unharmed."

"They have rights who dare maintain them,"

and many a long century will go by ere the world loses the necessity for the old fighting instincts. One may well believe that the men who are fighting corrupt political gangs in their manhood, fought the gangs of the next street in their youth, and so learned the fighting habit.

Fighting is like plaguing in being an anti-social impulse. Unlike the latter, on the other hand, it possesses great pedagogical value. There is nothing like a fight between individuals to teach physical and moral courage, self-reliance and self-control; and when, in addition, the battle involves the honor of the gang, it becomes one of the most forceful of lessons in the social virtues. Either the fighting experiences of boyhood, or the fighting instincts which persist into adult life, or both together, make it impossible for men ever to treat one another as rudely as women often do.

Nevertheless, this feature of boy life does present troublesome problems. We come suddenly upon two boys fighting, and our grown up standards of conduct compel us to separate them. Afterwards, when we think it over, we are apt to regret that we happened to appear on the scene at that precise moment. It would have been just as well, we realize, for all parties, if the battle had been fought out.

As a rule, boys do not need to be encouraged to fight,—but neither should they be discouraged without careful consideration both of the boy and of his environment. There are times when every boy must defend his own rights if he is not to become a coward, and lose the road to independence and true manhood. The boy who is a bully needs a good thrashing—and usually gets it. The strong-willed boy needs no inspiration to combat, but often a good deal of guidance and restraint. If he fights more than, let us say, a half-dozen times a week,—except, of course, during his first week at a new school,—he is probably over-quarrel-some and needs the curb. The sensitive, retiring boy, on the other hand, commonly needs encouragement to stand his ground and fight. Time is well spent with boys of this sort, in teaching them to wrestle and box. Such encouragement and instruction may spare them the lifelong habit of timidity.

On the whole, for the average boy, the ground is pretty well covered by two rules of an old sea captain on the Kennebec River down in Maine:—

"Rule 1. If my boy comes home and has given a smaller boy than he is a licking, I give him another.

"Rule 2. If my boy comes home and has let a bigger boy than he is give him a licking, I give him another."

I ought to add, by way of commentary, for the benefit of readers of the peaceable sex, that in the technical vocabulary of the human male, to let another person "give one a licking" does not mean to be beaten after a brave fight, but to "take it lying down," that is to say, without putting up a decent resistance against overwhelming odds. According to the code of honor of Boyville, when one is struck he is to strike back. It is not for him to consider the outcome.

The bellicose impulse, furthermore, tends gradually to limit itself, as successive combats make it more and more clear which boy can "lick" which, and as the boys slowly learn justice and toleration under the discipline of associate life. Like most of the anti-social instincts of boyhood, it is essentially transient; if left alone, it will largely cure itself. Circumstances over which we do have a great deal of control, however, fix these instincts as habits. It is our duty to see that they do not, but the fighting impulse ought to die a natural, not an artificial death. To us is applicable, therefore, the parable of the tares among the wheat. We shall do well to keep our fingers off the tares, except when we are pretty certain that in gathering up the tares we shall not "root up also the wheat with them."

CHAPTER VIII

THE MANAGEMENT OF THE PREDATORY IMPULSES

Transitory nature of instincts— Acquisitiveness the basis of boys' thieving— Selflimiting quality of stealing— Effect of collections— Of common property— Cure of thievery must regard origin— Practical hints— Effect of gardens and shops— Unconscious element in anti-social impulses— Unfortunate position of city boy— Analysis of reasons for theft— Removal of specific causes— Summary of two chapters on anti-social gang activities and their cure.

WE are to look upon the gang as an association essentially instinctive. The boy at a certain age joins a gang, the gang pursues a definite set of activities, from motives that are primarily irrational. The boy is simply made that way. His behavior has the same instinctive basis as the acts of any other wild creature.

It is, so the psychologists tell us, a peculiarity of instincts among the higher animals, and especially of the instincts of mankind, that they are essentially transitory. They arise at the proper period of existence, persist in some cases only until the acts which they inspire have time to become habits, and then fade away. The squirrel born in a cage tries to bury nuts in the tin bottom. He tries it once or twice, and fails. He does not try it again; and probably would not, even though he returned to the woods. The tame beaver which builds its dam of chairs and umbrellas across the parlor floor, does it only once. The hen which cackles distractedly when her first brood of ducklings takes to the water trots calmly off to the pond with her third or fourth. But the duckling, kept away from the water for the first weeks of its existence, fears it forever afterwards.

So it is with these human instincts. They arise at early adolescence; they die down with the passing of youth. Meanwhile, they tend to develop into persistent habits of mind. Whether they shall so develop, and which shall persist and which die away, depends on the boys' surroundings and education.

Consider, for example, the special human instinct which we share with only a few of the brutes, the instinct of acquisitiveness. It is the basis of most of our adult frugality, and of the institution of private property. Too little of it makes us spendthrifts; too much makes us misers and kleptomaniacs; with just the right amount we become solid citizens and taxpayers.

Unquestionably, acquisitiveness is instinctive in boys; witness the contents of their pockets, and their collections of all sorts of useless truck. They steal things to eat and to provision their camps, with about as much attention to the morals of their acts as the squirrel who secretes nuts or the dog who buries his bone. They are continually appropriating articles which they cannot possibly use, merely for the sake of possessing them. It was a wise mother and a good psychologist who, when her cake became too dry to put upon the table, used to "hide it away for the children to steal."

In the adolescent boy this entirely natural instinct usually shows itself as a desire to steal, which is normal but not proper. On the whole, the gang does encourage stealing; forty-nine of our sixty-six gangs report this form of predatory activity. We all did it as boys, and most of us have grown up to be fairly honest men.

For there seem to be inherent forces in the gang itself that tend to check stealing. For one thing, both example and emulation among the members of a gang reinforce the impulse to form collections of shells, postage stamps, butterflies or minerals, and these in a natural and wholesome fashion satisfy the acquisitive instinct and turn it away from theft. The common property of the gang, too, its wood hut or clubroom with their furnishings, the bats and balls and other common tools of the gang probably act in the same way. Doubtless, too, the boys' grief when a hostile gang wrecks their property or runs off with their bats and balls reinforces powerfully the law of *meum et tuum*. Certain it is that experienced educators regard as vastly more serious the case of the lad who goes off to steal by himself for his own profit than that of the one who steals in company with his fellows and for the advantage of the gang.

The predatory activities of the gang do, then, in no small measure, tend to cure themselves. So far as they do not, they will naturally have to be put down by force in the interests of law and order. Yet even while we are curtailing these inconvenient activities, we ought never to forget that the stealing of boys is too natural and spontaneous to be, for them, a sin. Selfishness, disloyalty, cowardice, gluttony, are far more serious matters, for these are unnatural vices which grow worse with time. In putting down the anti-social gang activities, as of course we must, let us do it as psychologists, with an eye to the genesis and the nature of the disease which we combat. The impulse to steal is not primarily an instinct to take, but an instinct to acquire. What the boy desires is to secure property by some effort of his own. The raft and the hut which he builds, his collection of stamps and butterflies, the queer, useless treasures which he hoards, all these are the objects of his acquisitive instinct, quite as much as are the things that he steals.

The moral is clear. We may keep the boy from being a thief by making him a collector, and by making him an artisan. We help him to satisfy his natural desire for property in one way, and we check his tendency to satisfy it for himself in another. In the same way, so far as his thieving grows out of a love for excitement and adventure, as it undoubtedly does to a far greater extent than we commonly realize, the rational device for stopping it is to satisfy his desire for excitement and adventure in some other way. If, then, we encourage the boy to make collections of whatever he may be interested in, and give him some other experiences as delightful as "getting the chase," we shall have removed two of the chief causes of his thieving at all.

The creation and possession of property of one's own tend also to check the impulse to meddle with other people's in yet another way. I recall the case of a little Greek boy who had been smuggled into this country as a slave at a bootblack stand, and almost immediately after committed to a State Reform School for stealing. The boys at this school have each a little garden spot of their own which they plant and weed and tend and watch, and finally produce, among other fruits of their labors, melons. This little Greek had one melon plant on which in due season appeared a single tiny green watermelon. Never did a mother care more tenderly for her babe than this boy for his watermelon plant, and its single melon grew responsively. One day in the fall the little farmer said to his instructor, "Shall I pick my melon to-day?"

"No," was the reply, "you had better leave it one more week."

The next week when the boys went out for their gardening that single melon had disappeared. The little owner, with difficulty keeping back his tears, went sadly back to the schoolroom and asked to be permitted to see the Master.

"Do you remember," he said, "my watermelon?"

"Yes, indeed I do. What about it?"

"To-day when I went out to work in the garden, it was gone!"

"I am sorry. You have taken good care of that vine."

"Yes," returned the boy, "but I have learned a good lesson by it. I have learned never to steal any more."

"How did you learn that?"

"I have found out how much people are hurt when they have their things stolen."

The boy has, indeed, learned his lesson, for he has gone out from the Reform School to lead an honest life. All boys are fundamentally alike, and this same appeal to the sympathetic imagination must always remain our chief reliance in combating the predatory and destructive impulses of normal boyhood.

Let the boy, then, have property of his own which he has acquired by his own effort and you have taught him the great lesson of respect for the property of others. The boy who plants potatoes, hoes them, kills the potato bugs and harvests a bushel of potatoes, has gained a sufficiently correct sense of the value of potatoes so that he will not, as I have seen a gang do, dig up a poor man's winter stock of food just to see who could throw a potato farthest. The boy who makes a tool chest or a table can estimate the value of manufactured articles, and generally has a deep respect for well made furniture. One of the essential and fundamental elements in training for honesty and respect for property has been sadly neglected in our schools. A new era of promise is fast approaching when all boys and girls will receive a thorough training in handicraft and the still more valuable moral training which goes with it. Fortunate, indeed, and in more ways than one, is the boy who has learned in his teens the value of common things by the actual production of them.

It is well, also, for a boy to have a carpenter's room where he can use saws, hammers, and knives. If at Christmas time each year one good, useful tool is presented to a boy, by the time he reaches the gang age he has a useful kit in which he takes great pride. Then, too, this room often becomes a very good meeting-place of the gang, so that the boy's companions also turn naturally to making for themselves some of the objects which they require for their collective activities. Thus the gang itself not only contributes to the boy's manual education, but in a very real sense helps to tie the boy to his home.

It is especially important in dealing with these predatory and destructive instincts of the gang, to bear always in mind that they are thoroughly natural and inevitable. Every one of us men used to steal when we were boys; even Henry Ward Beecher confesses to having "swiped" sundry desirable objects "off" his Uncle Samuel from the Charlestown Navy Yard. "The man who says he never did it, does it now." The object of our training should not be to root out the instinct, but only to prevent its developing into a habit before it has time to die down of itself.

I was much struck with the thoroughly unconscious nature of these anti-social impulses by the case of a boy under my charge, who came to me for permission to go off into the woods with his gang during school hours. He told me in the most matter-of-fact way that they had just discovered the meeting-place of another gang, and they wanted permission to go there while the other gang was at school, loot their property, and destroy their habitation. It struck these well brought up boys that this highly piratical expedition was the only possible reaction on that particular fragment of their environment. It had not occurred to one of them that it was possible to let the other gang's property alone. The other gang, moreover, had carefully hidden their abiding place, taking it for granted that any other boys who discovered it would put it to sack.

Curiously too, the members of the two gangs were perfectly good friends, and neither looters nor looted would, apparently, have cherished the least grudge against the other. They were simply living up to their boy nature with no more thought of the reason for their acts than when, as children, they used to eat the paint off their Noah's ark, or when later, as young men, they will dance attendance on the girls whom they now despise.

It is important, too, for the parent, and still more for the teacher and the social worker, not only to recall his own youth and to be as charitable as his station in life will allow, but to remember in addition that in one way the city boy's environment is more against him to-day than ever before in history. The city boy takes fruit from a fruit stand, is arrested and given a record. In the eye of the law he is now a criminal, with an indelible smirch on his reputation.

If we elders had been treated after this fashion in our home towns and villages, who of us would lack a criminal record? We had a chance to steal fruit out of the orchards; and boylike, we preferred to steal sour apples from a mean neighbor rather than take sweet ones as a parental gift. The owner caught us, not the policeman; and after the dust had been thoroughly removed from the seats of our breeches, we were given a new start, none the worse. The consequences of the two sorts of theft are out of all proportion to their inherent sin.

Nevertheless, when all is said, stealing is a pretty serious matter, and it may help in handling the practical problem to follow out a little further the study of an earlier chapter, as to the reasons for theft. It appears from the boys' own reports, as well as from their chance remarks, that probably nine tenths of the objects stolen by youths before the age of sixteen are things to eat. The desire for food, therefore, is one of the most powerful contributory forces toward the formation of thieving habits. One obvious method, then, is to satisfy the hunger and thirst demands of boys. Well-fed boys from good homes do steal, but, other things being equal, the chances are vastly against the underfed. This aspect of the matter, unfortunately, takes us off into questions of economics and social science which, although important, have no place here.

Next to food in importance comes money, and objects such as lead, coal, wood, junk, and the like, which may be converted into money. Here again the remedy is obvious. Spending money for his reasonable desires, or a chance to earn it, should protect the boy from the second of the great temptations to theft. The parent who treats his boy to ice-cream or the circus, while he gratifies a natural desire, removes also a natural temptation.

Third in importance as causes of thievery come things to use,—saws, knives, hammers, and other tools, balls, bats, gloves, and the other implements of sport. In a sense the boy has a right to these things, as he has a right to textbooks and the other apparatus of the schoolroom. They are the instruments of his education, a part of his reasonable claim on society.

Last of our groups of things stolen come pets. All boys love a good dog; most boys like to house, feed and care for pigeons, rabbits, cavies, mice, almost any sort of pet. They steal food to eat, tools to use and money to spend; but they steal pets to take home and love. Here, surely, is a demand of boy nature that every parent ought to manage to satisfy.

In brief, then, we have in the three most conspicuous anti-social impulses of the gang—stealing, fighting and plaguing people—three independent elements of boy psychology, each with a separate genesis, and each requiring a different treatment for its suppression or cure. Plaguing people is a survival from the past, which was presumably useful once but certainly is so no longer. The impulse must be put down by force or removed by education before it fixes itself as a habit. The fighting impulse is also a survival, highly useful once and of great pedagogic value now. Too much belligerency needs to be curtailed; too little needs to be increased; the plain boy has just about the right amount, and needs a good deal of letting alone. After all, the warfare-varied-with-armed-neutrality of boyhood is nature's own great training-school for certain of the finest of the egoistic virtues.

Stealing is in still a different category. It arises from an instinct, useful in the past and still more useful now. The problem is to suppress the inconvenient manifestation without impairing the basal impulse. Seldom, therefore, is it sufficient merely to know that a boy is a thief. One must know why he stole, and why he stole this particular object rather than some other. Only then shall we lead him still to desire, while he ceases to covet.

CHAPTER IX

THE TRIBAL INSTINCTS AND THE WANDERLUST

Inherent goodness of the gang impulses now to be discussed— Balance of home and gang life— General nature of the problem— Wholesomeness and spontaneity of these interests— Their usefulness in training for work— Their religious aspect— Uses of Sunday— Control of the Wanderlust— Its imperiousness— Its dangers— Its good side— Practical suggestions— Excursions to interesting places and historic spots— Camping trips— Truancy— Limitations of athletics— Advantage of noncompetitive sports over games— Their value as permanent sources of happiness.

We have dealt thus far more particularly with the anti-social and predatory impulses of the gang, with the stealing and teasing and fighting, which, while we cannot call them wholly evil, are nevertheless to be rather checked than encouraged. With all their incidental elements of good, they must be essentially transitory. The boy may be allowed to steal and tease and fight; the man may not. The problem is to suppress the undesirable activity with as little damage as possible.

Now we pass to gang impulses which are inherently good. They may need guidance and occasional pruning; but even if left alone, they are likely, on the whole, to contribute both to the efficiency and the happiness of life. Such evils as they bring are incidental; they largely disappear when home life and gang life are perfectly adjusted to one another.

For there must be a pretty accurate balance between the life of the home and the life of the gang, if the boy is to get the best training out of both. If the boy stays at home too much, he is likely to become sissy. If he spends too much time with his gang, the wild and savage impulses of boyhood receive too much exercise, and he becomes wolfish. The boy must, for the most part, make his social adjustments for himself, and the safest time for doing it is while he is still in the home. Boys who have been kept too close, up to the time when they go away to make life for themselves, too often afford most striking lessons in how not to do it. In college and in business, under their unaccustomed liberty, they go all to pieces for lack of the education which they should have had as boys in the gang.

The problem of controlling the instinctive gang activities, therefore, resolves itself into a question of not too much. The home will best influence the gang by aiding its more wholesome interests, while to a considerable extent it shuts its eyes to the rest. Each man does, in his social development, pass through various stages of savagery, and instead of trying to crush out even the most objectionable of the tribal instincts of the growing boy, we ought rather to seek to satisfy them in such wise that he may pass through the lower stages into the higher as safely and as quickly as possible. As Froebel has well said, "The vigorous and complete development of each successive stage depends upon the vigorous and characteristic development of all preceding stages of life."

The way, then, to deal with the gang instincts is to gratify them. We have already seen that approximately three quarters of our gangs are wont to indulge in hunting, fishing, boating, building camps, going into the woods or to ponds, playing Indians, and the like. This is especially remarkable, as nearly all the gangs of our study come from the cities. In country gangs, these forms of activity are always present. With both city and country boys, they might be made of far greater service than they commonly are.

All persons who have camped with boys know that their interest in the outdoor world does not have to be kindled, but rather restrained and guided. There is never any difficulty about filling in the idle time of the gang with these tribal activities, while there is no doubt that the rugged experiences of tramping, mountain climbing, and camp life, of hunting, fishing, and boating, with the almost infinite forms of manual training involved, wherever the boys do their own cooking and camp work, and care for their own rods, guns, and kits, afford one of the best, as it is one of the most natural, forms of manual education. There is, besides, for the city boy, a training in resourcefulness and gumption which he can hardly get elsewhere. Moreover, under the proper sort of men leaders, this rough outdoor life furnishes the very best conditions for instruction in physical and moral hygiene.

Somewhat paradoxically, therefore, much of this gang play trains a boy to work. Play is work that one likes. But it is work, and it cultivates the same concentration and persistence as work, and often the same constructive imagination. Boys, moreover, often work hard getting ready to play; and by a little tactful guidance from their elders, they can be led through these play activities to the enjoyment of work, and into sound developmental occupations. Notice how in the Tennis Club, the boys, under the inspiration of Mr. M., the father of one of them, went camping on a lake, and for the sake of going fishing, built themselves their own boat. What better education in skill of hand than that boat-building could be found for a crowd of boys on a summer vacation; what better introduction to the joy of labor!

The life of the woods has, moreover, yet another important function in the development of a boy's inner life. I have often, in taking cross country walks with boys, attempted to switch out from among the trees into open meadow or pasture land to save distance. Over and over again, however, have the boys protested. "No, don't. Let's stay in the woods," they have entreated. I am inclined to believe that the religious life in boys has its natural birthplace in the forests, in the temple not made with hands, where their fathers have been worshiping these ten thousand years. If this be true, the Sunday School teacher might well, at times, exchange the benches of an uninteresting room for the spots where our race, from the beginnings of its existence, has been learning its lessons of piety and reverence.

Sunday is, in fact, the great day of the week, for or against the home. It is, as appears from the boys' reports of their activities, characteristically Nature Day; and there is a well-marked practice among boys, no matter what they may do through the week, to go off in groups into the country on Sunday. Parents who wish to keep control of their boys should recognize this natural impulse, and be their companions on their Sunday excursions. Family migrations, on the one day of the week when the father is free to go with his boys, would be an efficient means of keeping the home influence around the boy. Surely there can in this be nothing irreligious.

Such a practice would, moreover, powerfully aid the parent in controlling one of the most troublesome of gang instincts, the *Wanderlust*. The roving impulse takes a sudden rise at the dawn of adolescence, and then gradually subsides. Most red-blooded young men hear the call of the red gods in the spring; not a few remain vagabonds all their lives.

Certain it is that this strange *Wanderlust* of man has been a tremendous force in history. It drove the Angles and Saxons into Britain, the English into North America, and the New Englanders into the great West. The traditional Westerner is planning to sell out and move farther on. The mere sight of the horizon is a challenge; and the boy longs to repeat the ancestral experience.

In the normal boy, the migratory instinct is at times the most imperious of his impulses. Many boys are driven by it to run away from home; few, indeed, are there of us who have not made our plans to go—and then changed our minds. It commonly takes the combined influence of good parents, good teachers and good playmates to cool us down; and where the neighborhood spirit is lost, as it often is in city life to-day, or the home is broken by death or desertion, or made inefficient by drunkenness, ignorance, or poverty, there is little to check the boy's response to the old fret. Off, therefore, the boy goes, first by day, then by night. How far this running-away instinct contributes to delinquency, it is difficult to estimate, but certainly it is one of the greatest factors. About one boy out of every five in most of our large cities is arrested before the age of twenty-one; and in a considerable proportion of cases the beginnings of wrongdoing can be traced to early wanderings.

On the other hand, running away from home does not always result in permanent moral harm; while even at the worst, the boy gains a self-reliance which nothing else can teach. Often, too, the impulse, instead of growing with what it feeds on, tends to disappear with its gratification. There is something to be said also for giving the boy his fill of one sort of adventure before he is old enough for another.

As the migratory impulse is far too deep-seated and powerful to be altogether restrained, the only method is to indulge it under supervision and educatively. The boy should be taken on any sort of interesting trip. If the expedition involves some bodily hardship, so much the better. The son of a good home is usually made too comfortable, and unconsciously he feels the need of some more invigorating substitute for warm room and soft bed. When, therefore, nothing better offers itself, it often does a boy good to sleep out in his own back yard, with a dismantled revolver in his belt, and a lasso hung beside him on the clothes pole. He will probably not get much sleep, and he may catch cold; but the experience will be a powerful stimulus to his imagination, and at the same time will help, at small risk, to gratify a wholesome instinct.

The wise parent will take every opportunity to go on trips with his sons to city or country; the gymnastic instructor will arrange cross-country runs for his boys in spring and fall; and the school-teacher will plan nature-study walks, trips to historic spots, or visits to industrial plants, where, under a well-informed guide, the class will learn about manufacturing processes from the raw material to the finished product. All these persons are killing two birds with one stone. They are satisfying the runaway instinct, while at the same time they furnish the best sort of education.

In all sections of our land there are sacred historic spots, buildings, graveyards, battle-grounds, which help to keep alive the memory of noble men and women. There is a period in boy life when these have an intense interest; when the boy, eager for any form of experience or adventure, has his imagination powerfully stirred by whatever he associates with the adventures and experience of other human beings. I have often visited historic Concord with groups of school-boys, and though they were of all nationalities, I have yet to find one who could not be deeply impressed at the sight of Concord Bridge and the statue of the Minute Man. Teachers who were present, and told their pupils the story of what had happened on that ground, reported after their return the extraordinary interest of the boys' essays on their pilgrimage. The boys had seen with their eyes and the past had become real. Could there be any more effective method of teaching history, quite aside from the incidental satisfaction of a deep instinctive need?

If, in addition to such informative trips, the parent or teacher can go camping or tramping with his boys, then the climax is reached. Some pond should be selected with good boating, fishing, and swimming, and there ought to be a mountain near by which the boys can climb, camp on its sides overnight, and go to the top for sunrise. Such an experience will never be forgotten. Not only will it tend to kindle a lifelong interest in hills and mountains; in addition and more important still, the companionship in adventure gives the man a hold over his boys that nothing else can bestow. In the woods, on the mountain top and around the camp fire at night, come feelings of mystery, of awe, and of friendliness, to which the boy is at other times a stranger. Here is the opportunity for genuine moral and religious instruction. Better one straight talk under these conditions, than a whole year of lessons forced upon boys. Genuine morality and genuine religion are such deep and sacred and natural things that a little real inspiration lasts forever.

Probably, however, the most obvious and the most annoying aspect of the *Wanderlust* is truancy. It takes a shrewd teacher who knows boys, backed by a good home, to hold a boy in the schoolroom in the warm days of spring when the baseball fever is at its height. Most boys become thoroughly tired of the inactivity, restraint and monotony of the schoolroom; while the matter is by no means simplified by the fact that the teacher herself commonly belongs to the sex to which certain aspects of boy nature must be forever a closed book. Granted that truancy is not to be tolerated, we must never, in dealing with any actual truant, lose sight of the fact that truancy is not a sin. It arises from two coöperating forces,—the lack of adaptation of the schools to the needs of growing boys, and the determination of the boys to be true to their own nature. For one of these factors we elders are responsible; the boy is responsible for neither.

This is the day of athletics. The adult world has learned thoroughly the lesson that there can be no perfect physical development without the training which comes from the competitive and group games. Hardly less important, of late years, has been the emphasis of those who know boys best on the social and moral aspects of athletic training. The best boys' schools to-day provide for outdoor and indoor sports as carefully as for any other branch of education.

This lesson, I say, we have at last pretty well learned. We have not yet discovered, however, that the native impulses which lead a boy to baseball and hockey are only part of his equipment of gang instincts. The desire for athletic exercise which, at least for the favored few, is now being gratified at so great an expense, is no older and no more deep-seated than the desire for these activities which we have called, for lack of a better name, tribal and migratory. The boy needs diamond and gymnasium and running track. But quite as much he needs mountain and lake and river and forests. He takes a step toward manhood when he stands by his fellows through a hard-fought match. He also takes a step toward manhood when he sleeps alone under the stars.

In one respect, moreover, the boy who plays ball is at no small disadvantage in after life as compared with the boy who plays Indian. The athlete will play his favorite game while he is at school. He will get a thorough and wholesome physical training, and possibly some not especially wholesome notoriety. If his parents can afford to keep him four years in college, he plays there. Afterwards, unless he is especially fortunate, he does not play at all; and all his carefully acquired skill goes for nothing.

But the boy who has indulged wisely his tribal and migratory instincts has for the rest of his life a never-failing source of happiness. He has learned to love nature, and to delight in his own handiwork. To walk in the woods, to climb mountains, to own the little camp which succeeds to the place in his affections once occupied by the rude, gang-built hut, to travel,—these are among the permanent satisfactions of life. If we except the group of instincts which lead the young man to found a family of his own, and to which, at the gang age, the boy should be a complete stranger, the tribal instincts of boyhood, wisely gratified and trained, are probably the greatest single factor in a happy life.

CHAPTER X

THE INDIVIDUALISTIC ACTIVITIES AND THE GROUP GAMES

Education through games— Their social training— The problem of playgrounds— Example of the best English schools— Value of swimming— Opportunity and supervision— Skating and dancing— Their peculiar function at the end of the gang period— Theatre, circus, and picture show— Analysis of their influence— Wholesomeness of melodrama.

THE boy, we believe, likes to play ball, to run, to dodge, to throw accurately and hard, to hit any quick-moving object with a club, because for untold ages his ancestors have been getting their food and guarding their lives by swift running and quick dodging, by accurate throwing and deft hitting of moving objects with clubs. These are the natural activities of growing boys; incidentally they train the boy for the chief employments of savagery, and for some of the most valuable recreations of civilization.

All this, however, is more or less by the way. The great value of athletic games is the education they give toward essential qualities in our modern, civilized and work-a-day world. A judicious blending of work and gymnastics would probably bring about as high a physical development as would the same training supplemented by games; but it would stop there. Only sports, one may say only competitive sports, can bring about the perfect adjustment of hand and eye, the sense of "time," the quickness of resource, the steadiness under excitement, which mark the successful athlete. Games are the easiest, the most natural, the pleasantest means of acquiring certain highly valuable qualities; they are, in addition, almost the only means of acquiring certain others.

For we make a mistake when we think of athletic games as contributors only, or even chiefly, to muscular development and to soundness of body. Their most important function is to train the nervous system, the intelligence, and the will. As has often been pointed out, the successful athlete is not necessarily an especially strong man. He is a man who has learned to use his strength, whose nervous adjustment is precise, whose body responds perfectly to the demands of his will. The baseball field, in short, is one of the easiest roads to self-command.

But the playing-field has also an important social function. Games are really the great social events of boyhood; in them he learns the great art of getting on with his fellows. It is a curious sight to watch a group of little boys when they first begin to play ball together. Such wrangling and disputings as there are, such refusals to play unless each can have completely his own way, such protracted controversy over each least difference of opinion! Shortly, to begin with, each little boy takes his bat or his ball, and departs for home and sand pile. The next day they will play together a little longer. They are beginning to learn one of the great lessons of life, and by the time these boys have "made" their college team, their nice adjustment of nerve and muscle will be hardly more manifest than their utter conformity of intelligence and will. The erstwhile discordant group will have become a single instrument. The separate individuals will have been trained to coöperation.

Thus the playing-field confers both a muscular and a social education. While it is training the muscular sense, it is cultivating also the sense of human brotherhood, and the knack of getting on with other people. "Activities calling for coöperation and self-sacrifice," says Luther Gulick, "form the natural basis upon which a life of service can be built.... This life for others is far more probable, natural, and tangible, when it comes as the natural unfolding or development of that instinct which has its first great impulse of growth in the games of adolescence."

The wise parent, therefore, will look well to his sons' games for reasons which do not lie wholly on the surface. The money that he spends on bats and balls and mits is going toward their education, and in no other way will he get more education for his money. It will be recalled that one of the past members of the Tennis Club believed if he had remained in the gang, it would have saved him from the Reform School. This was an especially fine gang, and its goodness was in no small measure due to the same Mr. M. who took the boys camping. He saw to it that the boys had a place to play and apparatus to play with, and he used the gang in dealing with boys, as he probably used club and lodge and union in dealing with men, "for all there was in it."

The place to play is too often the point at which the boy's education breaks down. Consider the conditions in almost any house-bordered street in the more thickly settled parts of any large city. It is the breathing-space, nursery, thoroughfare, market, and playground for crowded tenements. Here the boys congregate and play, and come daily into conflict with the officers of the law,—the very worst possible education that can be given to a boy. This conflict causes enmity to spring up between the boys' gang and the organized government, where there should be coöperation and good will. The mischief-making tendencies which spring from this enmity land many a boy in the delinquent class.

Too often in our cities and villages the park is found near the centre, while the playgrounds are pushed to the outskirts, and relegated to vacant lots of good-natured or absent owners. Boys love best to play close to their homes, at the centres of interest, where they can be watched at their games. Experience shows that the boy will not commonly travel more than a short distance to his playground, even though he will go miles to a swimming-hole. Somehow the distant field is the enemy's country, and he has the vague ancestral dread of stranger's territory.

Wise, then, is the village or city that provides frequent small open spaces for neighborhood playgrounds. It helps to develop the neighborhood spirit which is so sadly lacking in a modern city, and it helps to meet a normal demand of boy life. Such an arrangement is also a far-sighted economy, since, to quote Lee, "the boy without a playground is father to the man without a job."

We ought not to forget that, from time immemorial, the education of boys has been almost entirely by spontaneous imitation of their elders, and by free play. The formal and compulsory portion of their education has, for the most part, been limited to various initiation ceremonies at puberty. Aside from these, boys have largely educated themselves.

The English public schools have for some years been organizing the boys' free play, and using it as an instrument to a definite educational end. An English school will run fifteen simultaneous cricket matches of an afternoon, each with only a handful of spectators. We in this country have hardly begun this method of education; and have not thus far advanced beyond the stage where a team of nine or eleven specialists play the game, and a hundred or two more spectators "support the team." The best schoolmasters to-day are using the group games as a valuable educational instrument and the tendency each year is to use them more and more.

But the schools which are doing this are few. At best they can hardly touch the tenth part of the boys who are now growing up, while even this tenth is precisely the portion which needs the training least. If the group games are to be made an efficient tool for the physical and moral training of our boys, it will have to be done by the municipalities,—and still more by the parents. Sooner or later, the time must come when an honest and enthusiastic game of ball will be recognized as an important factor, not only in the physical training of every boy, but in his intellectual, moral and even his religious training.

In addition, however, to these coöperating group games, the basis of which is, at least in part, the inherent instincts of boyhood, there still remain to be considered certain other gang activities, the instinctive basis of which is much less specific, activities which arise from the general impulse to do something interesting, and to do it in conjunction with one's fellows. These are gang activities, but only in the sense that the ordinary boy actually does take part in them as a member of the group, and while he might do the same things in solitude, actually seldom does do so.

First of these comes swimming. Swimming is perhaps the most popular of all sports during the summer season. The adolescent boy has a craving for the water, and, if not checked, will remain in it for half a day at a time. It is probably, on the whole, the safest way for most boys to get their necessary exercise in very hot weather, while at any time of the year it is, by general consent, the best all-round exercise there is. Moreover, except for the chance of drowning, it is the safest of athletic sports. Neither falls nor sprains nor broken bones nor any of the common accidents of ball field and gymnasium are possible to the swimmer. He cannot so much as strain a muscle against the yielding element.

For these reasons and because, of all interesting sports, swimming contributes most to the symmetrical muscular development of growing children, every community ought to provide some sort of convenient swimming place for its boys and girls. If it can manage to give them, in addition, a daily half-hour throughout the year, so much the better. Even an artificial swimming-tank is not especially expensive, when one considers to what large use it may be put. It would certainly be a great improvement if there could be in every public playground a children's swimming-pool, two or two and one half feet deep, in place of the dirty and useless wading-pool one so often sees.

Natural pool or artificial tank, however, every swimming-place ought to be under the supervision of the right kind of man. He ought to be a teacher, for the modern swimming-strokes are by no means easy to get exactly right, and boys seldom pick them up correctly for themselves. His chief function, however, should be to keep the moral atmosphere of the swimming-place clean and pure, for here if anywhere the tone of the company is likely to drop. Boys in their games keep pretty closely to associates of their own age and station in life, but the swimming-hole takes in all ages, and its society is apt to be somewhat too democratic.

While, however, the careful parent will take all reasonable pains to avoid any moral contamination at the swimming-hole, he ought never to allow his boy to fall into the other extreme of prudery. For healthy-minded men and boys the bathing-suit is at best a necessary evil, and trunks an utter absurdity. The last thing to be desired for a boy is anything resembling the modesty of a girl.

Of skating there is little that need be said. As simple skating or as ice hockey, it is, for three months in the year, the most valuable of winter sports in our Northern States, and one of the least expensive. It is a short-sighted community that does not keep cleaned and ready for daily use a safe, central skating-field. An active boy during the winter is often hard-pressed to find wholesome outlets for his energy, and the ice is often the only efficient rival of poolroom and saloon.

The skating-field is, besides, one of the natural places for the boy toward the end of the gang period to graduate into a new social life. The fresh, wholesome air, the brisk exercise, the sharp cold act together to discourage dalliance. Outside a better equipped home than one half of our boys and girls come from, there is no more wholesome place for them to meet one another than on the ice.

This last advantage, though at a long interval, skating shares with dancing; that is to say, if the dancing is properly conducted. A badly conducted dance comes near to being the worst environment in which a boy is ever likely to find himself. Boys at the gang age, however, except toward the end of the period, seldom care spontaneously for dancing at all. On the whole, probably, the wisest plan is to respect the natural impulses of the average boy and to discourage much departure from the type. The boy's manners will probably suffer, but the boy who is a perfect gentleman at fourteen usually has something permanently the matter with him.

As for theatres, circuses, and shows, for which boys have commonly a raging passion, it all depends on the show. All penny arcades and peep-shows are pretty certainly bad. Better keep the boy away. All performances attended predominantly by men are also bad, except athletic exhibitions and horse-races. The general run of vaudeville shows, with singing, dancing, and the like, are probably harmless enough in themselves, but they are commonly pretty inane, while the slight demand which they make on the voluntary attention cultivates a distinct trashiness of mind. Ordinary stage dancing, by women who are in no sense artists, is degrading both to performer and spectator, though, fortunately, to this influence the boy at the gang age, unless precociously educated, is nearly immune. At best, however, the vaudeville show, except its athletic turns and its exhibitions of trained animals, is a good deal foreign to the interests of boyhood; so that for various reasons, a taste for this sort of entertainment is something whose cultivation may well be postponed until extreme old age.

Circuses and other performances of like types are in a different category. Their feats of skill and strength and daring are a revelation to the boy, and a stimulus to emulation. The cowboys and Indians appeal strongly to his imagination, and help him to visualize the people whom he reads about in books. In many ways, these exhibitions are educative and valuable; such evil features as they sometimes have slip off the boy's mind like water from a duck. At the gang age, he is quite impervious to them.

Much the same is true of the moving-picture show, which seems to offer, just now, the pressing moral problem of the city parent. Where these are good,—and it is always the simplest matter in the world to find out whether they are or not,—they are likely to be very good indeed. They give the boy at second-hand all sorts of delightful experiences of travel and adventure. Where the films present scenes of industrial activity, historic settings, important contemporary events, interesting places, customs, or scenery, their educational value is often high. Like the circuses and "Wild West" shows, they help to gratify the migratory instinct, and to satisfy the boy's native curiosity and his desire to go out into the world and see things. I doubt whether we half realize how much the moving-picture show might be made to do for a boy if some one would show him what to look for, and tell him what it is all about.

On the other hand, the general drift of the moving-picture shows during the last few years has been in the direction of "playlets" of a rather stupid type, together with criminal and vicious suggestion for its own sake. This last is highly dangerous and ought to be controlled by strict censorship. Even here, however, we need to beware of attributing to the boy the standards and sensibilities of mature men and women.

As for the old-fashioned theatre, no one who studies the question without the old inherited church prejudices can think that the melodrama is dangerous. On the contrary, it furnishes, for the most part, a decidedly wholesome type of amusement. The usual form, in which the villain elaborates a mean, underhanded plot, only to be outwitted and defeated by the hero in the last act, produces a distinctly beneficial effect on the unsophisticated listener. It furnishes a vent for bad emotions, and at the same time gives a tonic shock to the rest. It does the boy good to see the paragon of all masculine virtues fight against all odds for the sake of the paragon of all feminine ones. The part that moves us elders to derision is precisely the part that has the most moral value for the inexperienced boy. What to us hints of evil, he simply does not see.

It is a suggestive fact that of the long list of plays which boys have told me they especially like to see, the great majority are good, with plenty of the fightings and shootings, villains and heroes and dogs, which boys like, and humor of a clean, if not especially subtle sort. To see such a play once a week will not hurt any boy. He will go home and reproduce it, as he reproduces the feats of the circus. And this reproduction is itself a promising activity of which much more use might be made in the boy's education.

In many ways, therefore, it is distinctly a social misfortune that vaudeville show and motion picture film have pretty much driven out the old-fashioned melodrama. Even at its worst, it had a coherent plot that enforced some sort of demand on the young hearers' attention, so that intellectually as well as morally it was superior to the types of entertainment which have supplanted it. All this, however, is from the point of view of the member of the gang. The effect of theatre going on older boys is a much more complicated matter.

CHAPTER XI

THE SPECIAL VIRTUES OF THE GANG

Psychologic value of the gang period— Biologic aspect of moral education— Loyalty the foundation of the gang— The boy's devotion to ideals— Mistakes of parents and teachers— Why all boys are not in gangs— Gangs are the natural training-schools for the social virtues— Pedagogic value of even anti-social acts— High social value of nearly all gang activities— This illustrated by typical rules of gangs— Gangs inculcate coöperation, courage, and other manly virtues— Late reversal of opinion with regard to the influence of gangs.

"THE boy problem," says J. J. Kimball, "is fundamentally not a personal problem nor a problem of intellectuality; not a moral problem, nor a psychological problem, though it may be all these,—but is, first of all, a biological problem." The instinct for activity is not new at the age of twelve, but it does take on new forms of expression. Some of these will begin and end with the gang period; some will persist through life, as work or as recreation. But during this especially active period, probably the most spontaneously active period of existence, there must be laid the foundations of all the more important interests of adult life.

There is a time for boys to learn to swim, hunt, fish, build huts, make boats, gather collections, play ball, love nature, work; or by neglect of this time, to lack interest in both work and play for the rest of their lives. There is a time also for learning the social arts and the social virtues. If this time passes with these lessons unlearned, it becomes highly improbable that they ever will be learned at all.

So far, then, as education is a biological question, it tends to resolve itself into the problem of utilizing the boy's instinctive interests as a basis for his formal training. This is especially true of his moral education. We take the boy at an impressionable age, an age during which he is probably more plastic than at any other time of life, either before or after. We can lead him through the group life of the gang, while the social instincts are being born and fashioned, into a social life of the highest ideals and devotion; or on the other hand, we may make him an unsocial or an anti-social being for life. The gang is a natural and a necessary stage in normal development. Carefully watched and wisely controlled, it is both the most natural and the least expensive instrument that we can employ to help our sons through one of the most critical periods of their lives. Nine tenths of the gang's activities depend on primitive instinctive impulses, which cannot be suppressed, and which need only to be sanely guided to carry the boy along the path which nature has marked out and bring him out at the end a useful citizen and a good man. The men who have been most successful in handling boys, men like Arnold of Rugby, Judge Lindsay and William R. George, are precisely the men who have appealed most powerfully to those boyish impulses.

Of all the gang-nurtured social virtues, loyalty and its allies stand easily first. The gang, indeed, exists only because of the loyalty of its members to one another. Without this mutual loyalty there could be no gangs. All the great leaders and successful trainers of boys use the lever of loyalty in reaching and holding their boys. Note the words of Judge Lindsay with Harry. "Judge! Judge! If you let me go, I'll never get you into trouble again!" "I had him. It was the voice of loyalty. I have used that appeal to loyalty hundreds of times since in our work with boys and it is almost infallibly successful." If we study the secret of the power of William R. George, we find him using the same strong lever. He trusts boys; he appeals to their loyalty; and he wins the toughest boys, with whom many others have failed.

This gang loyalty, however, is by no means a loyalty to individuals only; it is a loyalty also to ideals. The boy refuses to "squeal" under pressure, partly to shield his fellows, but still more because squealing is contrary to the boys' moral code. He joins the tribal wars, partly because, like the good barbarian he is, he loves his neighbor and hates his enemy, but quite as much because certain fightings are demanded by the gang's standard of honor. The moral education of the gang from the outside, therefore, consists, in part, of a deft substitution of the best ideals of the grown-up world in place of the crude standards of youth. But it must be deftly done and always, at any price, without violence to the immemorial code of Boyville.

Forgetting this, many an honest and zealous parent and teacher does irreparable harm when he finds the boy's moral code at variance with the man's. Unquestionably, for example, all good citizens, if adult, ought to inform the proper authorities of any violations of law and order, and to use their best efforts to bring offenders to justice. That we do not always take the trouble to do this, is an important reason why we are so badly governed. But the boy's code is precisely opposite. The good citizen of Boyville will shield the offender, and persistently refuse information to the authorities. It is far better to let boyish offenses go unpunished than to encourage boys to violate their native moral instincts; and all great schoolmasters have acted on this principle.

Less gifted teachers are often sorely tempted to listen to tell-taleing. It is often the quickest way to solve deep mysteries. Is it not better, however, to remain ignorant and suffer, rather than receive information from the boys' traitor? Three out of four of our boys admire the loyal playmate, and despise the traitor. When the teacher listens to volunteer assistants, she loses the good will of all the loyalists. From that day on, she has enlisted with the minority, who are the traitors and outcasts among their playmates.

The fond mamma is, naturally, the chief sinner in this regard. It often happens that dear Charlie comes in from his play and says, "Johnnie hit me." Mamma says, "I will attend to that matter," and she volunteers to go over and give Johnnie's mamma a free lecture on how to raise children. Charlie enjoys the excitement, and reports to his mother the next quarrel which he starts. If Charlie's mother had said, "Charlie, it takes two to make a quarrel, and when you get into trouble it is more manly for you to settle the matter without coming to me," his whole career of life might have been happier and better. Too often the mother's encouragement makes a decent and manly boy into a tell-tale and a coward, and so cuts him off from one of the great educative influences of life.

For the explanation why only three in every four boys are in gangs, instead of four in every four, is largely that the fourth boy is one whom the gang will not have. Some boys, of course, are solitary by nature,—sensitive, retiring boys who do not care for the rough life of the gang, but prefer to play alone, with one companion, or with girls. Some, too, grow up in isolated neighborhoods where there are few other boys of the same age. These lose, perforce, the education that comes in the gang. But the rest who stay out of the gang, stay out for the gang's good. They have been trained, often against their nature, to do violence to the gang's standard of honor. They fail to pass through the normal development of human males; they lack a fundamental virtue and their fellows will not trust them, boy or man.

In the gang, then, we find the natural time and place for the somewhat sudden birth and development of that spirit of loyalty which is the foundation of most of our social relations. We must, in short, look upon the gang as nature's special training-school for the social virtues. Only by associating himself with other boys can any youth learn the knack of getting on with his fellow men; acquire and practice coöperation, self-sacrifice, loyalty, fidelity, team play; and in general prepare himself to become the politician, the business man, the efficient citizen of a democracy. Nature, we must believe, has given the boy the gang instincts for the sake of making easy for him the practice of the gang virtues. It may well be questioned whether any association of state or church or neighborhood or school or order has had a greater influence over the lives of most of us men than had the dozen or so of boys who were our intimate companions between the ages of twelve and fifteen.

We must not forget that the instinctive vices of the gang tend largely to be self-limiting, so that the boy, even if left entirely alone, would outgrow most of his faults. Not so with the gang virtues. The impulses to loyalty, fidelity, coöperation, self-sacrifice, justice, which are at the basis of gang psychology, are powerfully reinforced, as we have already seen, by nearly all the typical gang activities.

Even collective stealing is a lesson in coöperation. Thieving expeditions are often definitely planned; one boy watches while the others steal; one engages the attention of the storekeeper while another annexes his property; one member of the gang plagues the victim to get chased, and then the rest loot his goods. Most especially, however, in the group games of the gang do we find the most convenient tool for teaching many of the most essential social qualities. "In playing group games," says Joseph Lee, "morality is being born and the social man, man the politician, man the citizen; and it is my belief that in most instances this political or social man will get himself thoroughly and successfully born in no other way."

The steady pressure of gang life on the side of the social virtues appears strikingly in the rules and customs of the organizations.

"Put me out," reports one youth, "because I said one fellow didn't have spunk to play the leader." "Put a boy out of the gang for fighting when he didn't need to." "Put a fellow out once for fighting with another boy. The other fellow was in the right." "Never allow a big fellow to pick on a little one. We were against smoking." "Had to be at work when he comes into the gang; must pay his dues." "All stand up for a fellow in trouble." "Help each other out if we get into trouble." "If anybody picked on one of our fellows, we would fight them." "If a fellow didn't divvy up, we started fighting with him." "Put a fellow out because he wouldn't take his share of expense." "A fellow wouldn't share up, so we fought him." "Put three out for bossing and running the place." "No fellow ever told on us. One fellow was caught. He stayed in Charles Street jail three months before the rest of us were caught."

Or consider the following unwritten laws of various gangs as a preparation for a law-abiding life. "If there was a dispute, leader settled it. If two fellows were fighting for a thing, he took it away from them and gave it to another fellow. In playing dice, chuck the fellow out who made the dispute." "I was leader. Would settle disputes. Would say whether it was right or not." "Quarrel for five or ten minutes, and then ask N. to settle it. We would be satisfied with what he would say." "The officers would most always settle the disputes. Talk it over, get circumstances, then settle it." "One of the bigger boys would settle it. They would stop the fighting." "If we had disputes, we would vote on it. One who would get majority, to him we would leave it go." "Get a fellow who could keep things to himself." "If he knew enough to keep still, let him come in." "If he was a good guy and round the corner every night, after a while let him in if he was not a squealer."

A "squealer," be it observed, is one who, being caught in an escapade, tells on the rest to save his own skin.

Disloyalty is the one unforgivable offense in boyish eyes, the one crime which inevitably leads to expulsion from the gang. "If he went against us, call him a back-biter. Chuck him out." "Put a fellow out for squealing on them." "Put him out because he would run off when needed to fight."

Among twenty-one boys who had been expelled from their gangs, eleven were put out for disloyalty, three for fighting in bad causes, and but one each for all other reasons. There is no other institution on earth that can take its place beside the boys' gang for the cultivation of unswerving loyalty to the group.

Close beside loyalty and fidelity, come the related virtues of obedience, self-sacrifice, and coöperation. The boy who will not obey the captain cannot play with the group. Baseball and football are impossible without coöperation, and they demand constant self-sacrifice of the individual to the team. The gang fight, brutal and useless as it commonly is, also calls for the highest devotion. It is fought, not for personal ends but for the honor of the gang. Often the fight is to redress the wrongs of another member of the gang; not infrequently it is on behalf of a younger brother of some member. In the great battle between C—— and E—— in which nearly a thousand boys took part, the *casus belli* was the wrongs of the little C—— lads on whom the E—— gangs had been "picking" beyond custom.

After all, there is nothing finer in all our human history than the loyalty of men to comrade and chief, to regiment and king and country, and their obedience even unto death. The Old Guard at Waterloo, the Spartans at Thermopylæ, the Boy on the Burning Deck, the Roman Guard at Pompeii, Horatius, Arnold von Winkelried,—who of us was not brought up on these stories? The manly virtues are instinctive in proper men, but men first learn their practice in the gang.

Almost every activity of the gang is a lesson in coöperation. Not only the group games and the fighting, but the peaceful tribal occupations,—the hunting, fishing, exploring, hut-building, swimming, skating,—all have to be done more or less in common. Tact, adaptability, skill in getting on with one's fellows, are among the minor virtues of the gang. So, too, is the spirit of democracy, for the gang is as little snobbish as any human group. It puts a premium also on strength of body, while most of its typical activities involve wholesome physical exercise which most boys would hardly undertake alone.

Last, but by no means least, of the gang virtues comes courage. Now courage and self-reliance are partly a matter of habit. One simply gets accustomed to danger, and so meets it without fear, knowing that he can take care of himself. Baseball and football are both brave games. The boy who is afraid to get his shins kicked, or to stand up to bat against a swift pitcher, has no place in either. Fighting often demands high courage, especially in group fight, where one cannot stop to pick an opponent of his own size but must stand his ground against all comers, little and big. Then there are also the "stunts" and "dares" which the members of the gang give one another. These also are a constant incentive to bravery. The coward is a social outcast who has no place in the gang; but the timid boy stands to have his timidity shamed and practiced out of him. For the naturally brave boy in the gang, courage soon becomes a fixed habit.

Considerations such as the foregoing are rapidly bringing about in the minds of educators, social workers and enlightened parents a radical alteration of opinion with regard to the nature and influence of boys' gangs. The time was when it was the nearly universal opinion that all gangs are bad and should be broken up as quickly as possible. This opinion, it must be admitted, is still that of a considerable majority of persons.

Of recent years, however, we are coming to see that this older attitude is not only false but futile. Man is a social animal, the social spirit in him has had a very long history, and the fundamental social virtues which support the complex structure of our modern civilization have been built into man's nature through thousands of generations. The little boy is an extreme individualist; somewhere he must be born again into the world of social coöperation. For the beginning of this new life, the gang seems to be the natural place. It is through the gang and by means of the gang that the modern educator and the modern parent will train the growing boy to his part in the collective life of the community.

CHAPTER XII

THE GANG IN CONSTRUCTIVE SOCIAL WORK

The Boy Scouts— The sound psychology of the organization and its relation to the boys' gang— The Church— The psychology of religious training and its practical method— The Sunday School— The Home— Prerequisites of good gangs— Families should unite to provide these— The Boys' Club— The Playground— The Summer Camp— its common failings— Suggestions for the improvement of these— Proper subjects for study in camp— Special fitness of instruction in hygiene and morals.

The Gang and the Boy Scouts

Of all present-day organizations for the improvement and the happiness of normal boyhood, the institution of the Boy Scout is built at once on the soundest psychology and the shrewdest insight into boy nature. The Scout Patrol is simply a boys' gang, systematized, overseen, affiliated with other like bodies, made efficient and interesting, as boys alone could never make it, and yet everywhere, from top to bottom, essentially a gang. Other organizations have adopted gang features. Others have built themselves around various gang elements. The Boy Scout Patrol alone is the gang.

How thoroughly this is true, appears at once in the actual details of the scout's training. He must learn to build a fire with two matches; to swim a specified distance, and to take a companion ashore; to handle and to care for, according to the situation, canoe or boat or horse; to find his way across country and through woods to a designated spot and back, within a specified time; to track a companion by his foot marks; and to spy upon a, constructively, hostile camp without being discovered. In short, he is taught to "play Indians" with a thoroughness and success which no unaided gang can approach.

Like the spontaneous gang, the patrol puts special emphasis on coöperation, loyalty, obedience, and honor. The scout is a soldier; he may discuss and argue and protest to his heart's content—afterwards. But he will obey first. The scout is a gentleman; whatever he declares "on his honor" is to be received without question. He is to stand by his friends, to respond to the call of any other scout. These are the simple rules of the organization, as they are the rules, written or unwritten, of every boys' gang that ever existed.

Most ingeniously does the scout's training feed his social instincts. He is taught all sorts of sign languages,—marks on the ground or in the woods that tell which way he has gone, where there is water, or the wrong path which those who follow him should avoid. He learns to signal with smoke and with flashes of sunlight from a mirror, to telegraph, to wigwag, to do semaphore signals with his arms. In all these ways he is given one of the most precious possessions of boyhood, the secret code which only he and his friends understand; while at the same time he is initiated into the great company of soldiers, sailors, engineers, explorers, railroad men, and other romantic adventurers who also comprehend these mystic signs. The ordinary gang would give the boy this same sense of solidarity with other boys; the patrol gives him in addition a contact with the world of men.

Incidentally, of course, the patrol, like any other gang, goes swimming and skating, plays ball and the other group games, has its local habitation and its stamping-ground. In these respects it is simply an especially good gang—as good, let us say, as the Tennis Club of our earlier reports. In one way and another, therefore, it does everything that the spontaneous gang does, and does it a great deal more interestingly. The whole Boy Scout movement is a shrewd and highly successful attempt to take the natural, instinctive, spontaneous boys' society, to add nothing to what is already there, but deliberately to guide the boy into getting completely just that for which he blindly gropes.

The obvious answer to the whole gang problem, therefore, is this: Turn your gang into a Boy Scout Patrol.

The Gang and the Church

If one were to give to an average boy a religious education which should be thoroughly psychological, and quite independent of any particular theological bias of those who had him in charge, one may fancy that method would be something as follows.

While the boy is still a child, before he arrives at the gang age, and while he is still educating himself through his larger muscles and the cruder perceptions of his sense organs, he should attend a place of worship with an elaborate ritual. The child at this stage is developing rapidly his acquaintance with sound and color, and is learning to coördinate the larger movements of his body. He is in the period of drum and trumpet and the running-games, so that the appeal of the church service to eye and ear, the processions and recessions, the movements of clergy and choir, even his own changes of posture as he sits, stands, or kneels, all fit in with the strongest interests of his secular life. The ornate ritual, therefore, with short sermon or none, makes precisely the appeal to which the way is most open. This, then, is the time to instill reverence through the ministration of the church.

Now, reverence, which is fundamental to religion, is itself founded on the muscles. Just as we are angry, so the psychologists tell us, because we clench our fists and snarl our lips, so we are reverent because we bow our heads. As one cannot be thoroughly angry so long as he keeps his hands open and makes himself smile, so he cannot tip back in his chair, put his feet on the table, and pray. The mood will not come till the muscles point the way. There are, to be sure, genuine conversions late in life, as there are miracles of other sorts. But the normal religious man is one who, in boyhood, at the period of life when he was establishing his other great muscular correlations, has been put through the movements of worship till they became habits. We make a devotee, in short, precisely as we make a musician or an athlete.

With the advent of the early gang period, however, the boy's relation to the world undergoes a sudden change; and naturally his attitude toward religion will alter with it. He who once babbled to any listener becomes reserved. The desire for sensation is now replaced by a desire for experience. Woods and sea and the greater forces of nature are now the objects of his religious instincts. His interest is in the creation, and the proper channel through which to instill reverence is friendship with Nature. The child has become a savage, and he worships the red gods.

With the later gang period and the stage which immediately succeeds it, comes normally the veneration of a hero. By this time the boy leader of the gang has emerged from the general ruck of its members, and his word has become law. Now is the time of greatest influence of the man leader—father, trainer, scout-master, pastor, or older friend. Now, for the first time, the boy, beginning to find himself, becomes capable of special and enduring friendships; probably, too, he falls frequently in love. In short, his one absorbing instinctive interest is in personality.

The proper minister of religion at this stage is no longer the ritualist, but the inspired preacher; and the less of form and ceremony and church millinery, the better. The boy's instinctive hero-worship turns him toward any prophet of righteousness whose theme is the moral life, the duties of this present day, and "the religion of all good men." At the age of sixteen, he normally experiences conversion.

After that comes, of course, the period of intellectual skepticism; and when that is by, the erstwhile boy settles down to the enduring faith of his manhood, in which all the religious experiences of youth have their part. For the rest of his life, few changes will go deeper than mere matters of taste and opinion.

We, however, are concerned only with the boy at the gang age. His problem is simple in theory,—and anything but simple in practice. Preaching at this stage does him little good, nor does form and ritual. He should already have fixed his habits; now is the time for ideals and dreams. The boy is instinctively a nature worshiper, and the one essential thing is to get him out of doors in company with the right sort of man. This is no time for bible or hymn book; there is time enough for these both before and after. What the boy wants now is to learn about life. To set him at Sunday School lessons under a woman teacher is a pedagogic crime.

We need, then, in church and Sunday School, for influencing boys at the gang age, simple manliness far more than we need either learning or piety. If we have done our full duty by the boy up to the age of twelve, and if we are prepared to go on with his formal religious instruction after he passes sixteen, we may safely leave the welfare of his soul for these intervening four years to nature and to the unconscious example of almost any good man. For boys at the gang age, I would choose as a Sunday School teacher the sort of man who makes a good scout-master, even if he himself made no profession of religion whatever, rather than the stanchest pillar of the church who has forgotten his boyhood, or than the most angelic maiden lady that ever lived. This is one of the cases where the children of this world have been appreciably wiser than the children of light.

The Gang and the Sunday School

Of the gang and the Sunday School, as apart from the church, little need be added to what has already been said. The common mistake is to pick out the proper number of boys, of about the proper age, but with small regard to their other qualities, and out of these to form a class. The result is, that unless the teacher possesses most uncommon gifts, the class never has any coherence. It is not a natural group, and it never develops the internal structure of a real gang. There may be too many natural leaders. There may be too few. Or the class may combine fragments of rival gangs that are "licking" one another on sight, six days in the week. More commonly, the class contains a considerable fragment of one gang, with one or two individuals out of several others, and perhaps an occasional out-lier who belongs to none. The remainders of the broken gangs are in other Sunday Schools. Thus the class remains always at cross purposes with the boys' native impulses; and rarely, therefore, wins their instinctive loyalty.

The remedy is the method of the Boy Scouts. Organize your Sunday School classes on the basis of natural affiliations. Found each on some spontaneous group. Add, if you think it wise, some boys whose ganginess is less developed. But don't put fragments of well defined gangs together. Then, if some of your own boys follow their gangs to other schools, you can trust that, in the end, enough others come to you to even up. The essential matter at the gang age is the boys, not the denominational interests of their parents.

The Gang and the Home

There are three primary social groups in a modern state,—the family, the neighborhood, and the play group, which is, for our purposes, the gang. The second of these has become pretty much extinct in our cities, in spite of the efforts of settlement workers to preserve or revive it. The typical city dweller does not know the people in the next house by name, and views with instinctive hostility the family in the neighboring flat.

This really leaves only the home and the gang for the boy's informal training in citizenship, so that these two need more than ever to stand together; and although in essence, this entire book is a discussion of the ways in which the home may utilize the gang, there still remain one or two points that are worthy of special emphasis.

A thoroughly "good" gang, to do its best work, ought to have a meeting place, a shop, a man leader, a playground, and a stretch of wild country for its members to roam about in. All these, in some form or other, the home ought to furnish. Allowing for two or three pairs of brothers in the same gang, each group will commonly represent at least a half-dozen households; and these, among them, ought to be able to provide the gang with the essentials of its profitable existence. Somewhere in those families, there should be at least one spare room, one large back yard, and one father, uncle, cousin or big brother who likes boys. Somewhere in those families, there ought to be country relatives or the owner of some sort of a camping-ground.

The only thing, then, for a group of households related to one another through a boys' gang to do is to recognize frankly this relationship, and to live up to it. The father who has no room for a shop can put up the money for bats and balls; the mother who cannot stand the boys' racket can provide grub for the summer trip. Somehow or other, six reasonably well-to-do households, if only they will stand together, can always manage to give the gang about all it needs for its best efficiency.

What I especially urge, then, is that the good home shall recognize the good gang as among the most efficient of its allies. As the careful parent keeps an eye on school and church and social set, so ought he to keep his eye on the gang. He should make it his business to know, not only that his boy gets into the right gang, but that he enters it at the right age, neither too early nor too late, and that he graduates at the right time, after the gang has done its perfect work and more would be too much. He should see to it also—as I shall point out at some length in another volume—that the boy, being in the right gang, has also the right place in it, so that he gets his due training in the great art of making his will count in actions of other men. Most especially, as I have all along been pointing out, he should see that the gang as an organization gets its chance and lives its life, with its fitting environment and its proper tools.

The Gang and the Boys' Club

Unfortunately, however, taking the mass of boys as they come, about one boy in every two, either because of lack of room in his home, or because of sickness or death or poverty, cannot look to his parents for any aid in his group life. For him there remains the boys' club. The best of these are those which recognize themselves as mere adjuncts to the gang, which furnish a chance for wholesome exercise and play under the direction of a man who knows when to be blind and deaf, and for the rest lets the boys a good deal alone.

During the warmer months of the year, the city boy, for whom naturally the boys' club is designed, will spend his time out of doors. Playing field and swimming place, trips into the country on foot, with longer journeys by rail and trolley, keep the gang actively engaged in ways which are for the most part wholesome. Even the least desirable of them serve to work off the boy's abounding energy, and keep him from worse things.

AN INADEQUATE PLAYGROUND

The outdoor gymnasium is not enough

A MODEL PLAYGROUND

Boys at the gang age need room for the group games

The peril of the city gang comes with the cooler weather of fall, when the early darkness hides its doings, and any meeting place becomes attractive if it is warm. This is the time for the boys' club to capture the gang. The game is to keep the boys off the streets, and out of worse places, between the hours of four in the afternoon and ten in the evening. If at this critical time a boy can explode his energy in wholesome ways and amid good surroundings, the rest of the day will largely take care of itself. The gang demands a place to meet and to do things. This place will either be the home, the boys' club—or elsewhere.

The Gang and the Playground

In certain of its aspects the problem of the playground is not unlike that of the boys' club. Each exists primarily to give the boy opportunity of activity, spontaneous and largely self-directed, yet under supervision, adequate but not meddlesome.

The playground, however, is vastly the more important of the two. Our artificial city life fails, more than anywhere else, in its handling of boys. We have parks and boulevards and speedways, public baths and golf courses and wading-pools and sand piles, free museums and art galleries and libraries, not, to be sure, in any profusion, but often in number fairly adequate to the demand. The one thing our cities commonly lack is enough places where growing boys can indulge in a wholesome game of ball without getting themselves into some sort of trouble.

To be of any use to boys, a playground must be large. A small ground, with swings and teeters and sand piles, is for children. But the gang needs room to play the specialized group games against its rivals. How the city gang is to get this is another question, and one worthy of very careful consideration by those having the welfare of boys at heart.

The Gang and the Summer Camp

It might be inferred from what I have already written in praise of camp life for boys that I place the boys' summer camp high on the list of favorable environments for youth. This is by no means the fact. The typical summer camp, such as is advertised by the score in every magazine, is altogether too much an affair *de luxe* to be of much real value. It is too apt to be merely a school under canvas, or worse still, a summer hotel. So much is done for the boys that they lose all the training in skill of hand, in woodcraft, in self-reliance, in gumption, which a proper camp ought to give. Worst of all, they have little chance to "endure hardness." Life is nearly as soft as in the city; and for all the primitive manliness that the camp puts into them, they might as well have stayed at home.

Summer camps, also, for business reasons, are likely to be too large. The ideal arrangement is six or eight, or at most ten, boys who have already made themselves into a gang, with a man leader. A natural group, in short, with a natural man added on, is far superior to a selection on any other basis. If for any reason, the group must be larger, then there should be two or more men leaders, and provision for the group to break up into several natural gangs.

The best time to camp is late in the summer. Boys when left to their own impulses build their camps in the fall, urged thereto by as blind an instinct as that which sets the birds to building nests in the spring. Late summer is as near the natural building-time as the school system of civilization permits us to get; and besides this, the camping trip at the end of the vacation serves as the climax to be looked forward to all through the hot weather.

The two months' camp in the summer is based rather on custom than on experience or sound theory. Four short periods, during four different seasons, are far better than a single long stretch during one. Boys at the gang age desire ardently experience. That they get in fourfold measure, when to the common sports of summer are added hunting and trapping and nutting, expeditions on skates and snowshoes, fishing through the ice in the winter or in the first open water of the spring, and all the other rich and varied doings of the yearly round. It is any season but summer, also, for the touch of hardship which for every true boy is the salt of camp life.

As for formal instruction in camp, the less of books the better. Natural history, of course, there is, and the simpler handicrafts, and the various outdoor arts, from boat-building to camp cookery. Practical surveying may sometimes be conveniently managed, together with some of its attendant mathematics. There is often a chance, too, for a limited amount of physics, especially on the practical and the observational sides, and in the region between block and tackle on the one hand and the theory of the weather on the other.

But the one subject above all others for camp study is hygiene. Here is illustrated, practically and on a convenient scale, the entire subject of communal hygiene, from the obtaining and storage and preparation of food, to the disposal of waste, and the necessity of order and system in any sort of group housekeeping. As for personal hygiene, the white light that beats about a camp, where every act has to be done in public, reveals many a need for instruction on this side; while the frankness and naturalness of camp life make such lessons easy to give. Example, too, counts here as it rarely can where existence is more private. For public hygiene, therefore, and for private, a well-managed camp is an ideal school.

Most especially is a camp an ideal spot for instruction concerning sex. The candor and wholesomeness of camp life, the busy days and the solemn nights, the absence, one must confess, of one half the human race, all make for purity of heart. At no time, probably, can a high-minded man do so much toward setting a boy's feet along the narrow way.

CHAPTER XIII

THE GANG AND THE SCHOOL

The nature of the problem— Necessity of comprehending the gang spirit— Illustration from fighting and by an incident of real life— Difference between boys and girls— Boys' motor-mindedness— Practical hints— Importance of using natural groups— Illustrated by gymnastics— By nature study— By work in practical arithmetic— By other coöperative efforts— By pupil self-government— The important matter is to utilize the great passions of boyhood.

THE problem of the school, so far as the gang is concerned, is not so much to use actual gangs for the furtherance of its objects, as it is to use the underlying instincts of boyhood, which lead to the formation of gangs. These instincts normally lead the boy to associate himself with other boys in a gang and in this gang to pursue certain lines of activity. It is quite possible, in addition, to turn these gang instincts in the direction of the activities of the school. The emotional reaction of the boy toward his gang and its doings, can be extended, in part, to the school and its life.

For this purpose, the teacher must first of all understand the gang spirit. She is too apt, being herself a woman, to treat the boy as only a rougher and more troublesome sort of girl. She tends to interpret his acts as if they were those of a girl, and to forget how different in the two cases may be the inner meaning of the same overt deed. She errs, in short, by thinking of the boy in terms of her own woman's nature, when she should be studying him objectively as the quite different sort of creature that he actually is.

Take, for example, a rough-and-tumble fight. It is a rare woman who can see that as a boy sees it. She feels the brutality of the contest with something of the disgust with which she would view a case of fisticuffs between two women. She sees the dirt and blood, and she feels sympathetically the blows. What she does not feel is the "hour of glorious conflict, when the blood leaps, and the muscles rally for the mastery," the "joy of battle," the "seeing red," the decent, manly pride in taking one's punishment and "fighting it out as long as one can stand and see." The same teacher, because she is a woman, will face with steady courage an experience more dreadful than twenty fist fights rolled into one; and yet, because she is a woman, she may fail to see how long a step some bruised and disheveled youngster has taken toward manhood.

There are many acts of boyhood which, like fighting, seem brutal or depraved or absurd, until one makes out their instinctive basis, and realizes their inner meaning. Take, by way of another illustration, this case which fell under my own eye. A boy whose gang was "playing Indians" happened upon a flat piece of some dark red, hard-grained stone, and after days of labor fashioned from it a very respectable stone knife of the Neolithic period. As a tool, naturally, this stone knife was nearly worthless. As a piece of boyish handicraft, it was by no means without merit; and the maker had wrought it lovingly, with some vague instinctive feeling, I am sure, for the far-away times when a stone knife was an article of value to be handed down from father to son.

The boy carried this primitive tool in his pocket along with his other treasures, and showed it proudly to his companions, who, being themselves boys, admired and understood. One day, however, he left it on his desk, and returned to search for it, just in time to see his teacher pick it up and toss it contemptuously into the waste-basket. There it remained; for the owner was too grieved and hurt to take it out again.

So that teacher made an enemy where she ought to have made a friend. The trouble with her was that she did not know her business. Even if she could not understand all that the strange treasures of boyhood mean to a boy, that stone knife ought to have fairly shouted at her—Indians! Look out! To the seeing eye that fragment of stone bristled with meaning—the wild instincts of boyhood, its strange acquisitiveness, its joy in creation. To any reasonably sympathetic adult, it ought to have meant the opportunity to get a little nearer to one bewildered little soul.

The woman teacher, then, must learn to get outside herself and to see the boy as he is. She must study him as she would study any other wild creature. He has his own habits, his own instincts, and his own emotional reactions toward experience. These are to be studied in the spirit of a naturalist. Then, being understood, they are to be used.

Now, the boy, for our present purposes, differs from the girl in two respects. In the first place, he is vastly more active and motor-minded; and in the second, he is intensely and spontaneously loyal to a small but highly organized group of his fellows, in which his own individual will tends to become more or less merged.

The treatment of the first of these qualities of boyhood is perhaps a problem for superintendents and school boards rather than for individual teachers. One rejoices to see that, more and more every year, attention is being given to this aspect of boy nature. Manual training, industrial education, practical work of all sorts are relieving boys from the unnatural burden of acquisition and offering them instead their proper chance to do. Why is it, when we can all see so clearly the general superiority of the color sense in girls, we are so blind to the boy's preëminence in the muscular sense!

Much of this, I say, is not the problem of the individual teacher, who must, for the most part, conform to the school programme. Even here, however, an insight into boy character will help her in smaller matters, here and there, to handle the boy with the grain instead of across it. Outside school hours, there is sometimes opportunity for the teacher to enter into many of the activities dear to boyhood which I have already discussed. The excursions to interesting and historic spots, the nature walks, the visits to industrial plants, and the like, the value of which I have already emphasized, are for the most part quite within the range of most teachers. A few women of my acquaintance have even gone camping with their boys, and done it successfully.

The most important thing, however, is that the teacher, while she appeals at every turn to the natural activities of boys, shall always, so far as she possibly can, organize these activities on the basis of the boy's own spontaneous groups. When she cannot manage this, as in many cases she inevitably cannot, let her imitate in her artificial groupings the size, the quality, and the internal structure of the native gang.

For example, let us suppose that a teacher, fully alive to the motor-mindedness of boys, sets out to take special pains with the gymnastic work of her room. Suppose, too, she decides to follow a common practice and divide her pupils into squads or files, each with its separate leader. It will not do, in such a case, for her merely to pick out a half-dozen docile youths, and put each in charge of a random group. She ought, in the first place, to make her squads of about the same size as the gangs which the boys are forming of their own accord; and she should, in addition, select for her leaders, not the boys whom she happens to like or even the best performers, but the boys who are actually leaders in their own gangs. Then she should, so far as possible, let the leaders choose their squads, keep the groups together, and not make alterations without good reason.

By this device the squad becomes a gang, artificial and temporary, to be sure, but still enough of a gang to have some touch of the gang organization and the gang spirit. The amount of these will probably be small, but whatever there is is so much clear gain.

Or suppose a teacher goes in especially for nature study, and has her pupils make collections for the school, butterflies, beetles, minerals, it does not make much difference what,—stamps, if nothing else offers. By this means she appeals strongly to the acquisitive instinct, which, as we have seen, is especially strong in boys, and often the sole reason for their thievery. By this means also, since the collection is for the school, she appeals to the instinct of loyalty, and turns this powerful impulse of boyhood in the direction of the institution and of herself as a part of it. She may, however, without added labor, go still further. Let her organize the collecting on the basis of the boys' natural groups; let her work, in short, less with individuals and more with gangs. She can set one group to collecting one set of objects, and another group another set. But her groups should be like the natural gangs in size, and each should have one member, though not commonly more than one, who is already the natural leader in some permanent group. Thus, as before, the instinctive, spontaneous gang loyalty will unconsciously attach itself to the school and the school work.

The teacher, then, in dealing with boys, must learn to think in terms of gangs, as well as in terms of individuals. She must, in certain cases, go even further than this and think of gangs entirely, and not of individuals at all. Suppose, for her arithmetic class, she plans to take up as a practical problem, in mensuration and denominate numbers, the material which is, let us say, going into a dwelling-house in process of construction near by. Her thought should not be: I will send ten individuals to measure foundation or cellar or frame, and see which boy comes out best. She should think rather: I will send two gangs of five each, and see which gang comes out best. And these gangs should be as far as possible real gangs. The best device is to select the leaders, who, in turn, one need not say, must be boys whom the rough-and-ready election of their fellows has already elevated to a like post outside. These, then, should select their companions; and at once there results something of the gang structure and spirit. Then the rivalry of the gangs will make each boy expend far more effort than he would ever put forth for his own glory.

So it should be with any attempt to accomplish anything for the school. Is the room to be decorated for some occasion? The pupils as a whole should not attend to the room as a whole; nor should the pupils as individuals work as assistants to the teacher. Instead, the work should be divided into parts, and each part should be given to an independent group; to a natural group, as far as possible, but at any rate to a group under a natural leader.

Or is it a question of self-government, either in the schoolroom or on the playground? The head monitor, or whatever he is to be called, should pick his own assistants, and be responsible for their results. When the time comes for a change of authority,—it is well to have such change come periodically and somewhat often,—the whole group, prime minister and cabinet together, should go out of office at once, and another group take their place. That is the way men organize their industries and manage their governing. It may often be advisable to have the entire body of pupils elect the successive leaders; but the leader's assistants who are to work with him should be his own selection. Only thus can one make sure that they "will be in sympathy with the administration"—or, in other words, belong to the same temporary gang.

The main point, then, in dealing with school-boys at the gang age is to utilize to the full their natural groups. The little boy is an individualist, and we train him as an individual. But when later at the age of ten or twelve, the gregarious instincts begin to appear, the significant thing, the interesting thing, the unit with which, oftentimes, we have to work, is not the individual but the gang. For certain purposes, at this stage, we may ignore the boy and attend to the boy group. After sixteen the group dissolves, and once more we may take up the education of the individual.

The problem of the school is to utilize, to the full, the great moving passions of boyhood,—its loyalty, its self-sacrifice, its desire for coöperation, its thoroughgoing gregariousness. We do that best, in school and home and everywhere, when we learn to think of each boy in his gang relations, and to utilize these natural groupings as the basis of our artificial assemblages, and our guide in forming them.

Good citizens are sometimes quite as much the product of good gangs, as of good schools or good homes.

Lector House believes that a society develops through a two-fold approach of continuous learning and adaptation, which is derived from the study of classic literary works spread across the historic timeline of literature records. Therefore, we aim at reviving, repairing and redeveloping all those inaccessible or damaged but historically as well as culturally important literature across subjects so that the future generations may have an opportunity to study and learn from past works to embark upon a journey of creating a better future.

This book is a result of an effort made by Lector House towards making a contribution to the preservation and repair of original ancient works which might hold historical significance to the approach of continuous learning across subjects.

HAPPY READING & LEARNING!

LECTOR HOUSE LLP
E-MAIL: info@lectorhouse.com

9 789356 148239

Printed by Libri Plureos GmbH in Hamburg,
Germany